THE
IDEA
BOOK
FOR
MOTHERS

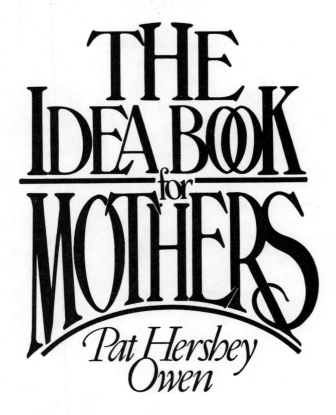

THE IDEA BOOK for MOTHERS

Pat Hershey Owen

TYNDALE HOUSE
Publishers, Inc.
Wheaton, Illinois

To
Terry Dwaine
Patricia Kathleen
Keith Alan
Alice Eileen
David Lee and
my mother
who inspired us all

Eighth printing, December 1986

Library of Congress Catalog Card Number 80-54033
ISBN 0-8423-1558-6, paper
Copyright © 1981 by Pat Hershey Owen
All rights reserved
Printed in the United States of America

CONTENTS

ONE
LEARNING TO LEARN

Creating a desire to learn begins when your child is
born and involves a vast amount of time and total
dedication. Even though it's true that the attention span of
small children is only a minute or so at a time, every
minute counts.

I believe that every child, when born, is endowed with
an intellectual potential (not a ready-made intelligence)
and this potential is crystallized by school age. Most
psychologists seem to agree that you can so train your
child during those first years of life, that by the time he is
school age, love of learning has become a habit. Many
children never really have an opportunity to want to go to
school. You see, in order for a child to be hungry for
the formal learning of school, his learning appetite needs
to have been stimulated.

Many children in America today are brought up in an
enriched environment. Why then doesn't this make a
difference in their mental abilities? Tests being run at the
Berkeley Laboratories prove that the growing animal's
psychological environment is of crucial importance for the
development of its brain. However, these studies overlook
one important distinction: an *enriched environment*
(abundant or valuable in possessions) and a *stimulating
environment* (to rouse to action or effort) are not one
and the same thing.

And therein lies a pitfall in our affluent era. We attempt to construct an enriched environment with our additional buying power, and deceive ourselves into believing that it does not matter that we have no time to create a stimulating learning environment for our children.

Through the years I've collected some stimulating ideas to help create a desire for learning in a child. Many I've used, some I've watched others use, but all of them help create within a child the desire to learn. I cannot emphasize too strongly that the key to early learning how to learn, is making it pleasant.

WORDS

Herbert Spencer once said, "Teach a child good English in the cradle and he will speak it to the grave."

I began talking to my children as soon as they began to notice me. I never handed or pointed to an object without distinctly saying its proper name. When they were big enough to watch me as I went about my various activities, I told them what I was doing, by repeating the words over and over again. "Mother is sweeping the floor," I would say. Or, "Mother is cutting carrots." I literally "bathed them in the sound of words" (a borrowed phrase I like). Although at first your child does not understand your words or what you are saying, he feels secure in the warmth of your attention and will early begin to comprehend conversation around him.

Before my oldest son was two, I had begun teaching him his letters. I hung brightly colored A's, which I had cut out of construction paper, around the walls of his room. Before his nap, we would point to each cut-out saying, "Red A, yellow A," etc. Gradually I added succeeding letters until he knew all the capital letters. We then started all over with the small letters. A bonus to this game was that it made naptime a looked-forward-to event.

After the alphabet was learned, we began to build words. We took letters off the wall and put them in a box. Every day we would build three words using the same three letters, and using the same word several days at a time. For example, we set Terry's stuffed dog, bear, and toy car on the floor with the proper letters leaning against them. He quickly learned to identify and "read" the names of his toys this way.

Each of these small steps (for the parent) is a giant step for the child. And each step helps the child master his language by laying a foundation on which conceptual thoughts are built.

Psychologist Edward Tolman said, "Speech is, in any really developed and characteristic sense, the sole prerogative of the human being." If this is true, it befits us to stimulate understanding and speaking as soon as the child has comprehension. Apparently, language determines how the environment is perceived, how perceptions are organized, and what kinds of abstract concepts can be invoked. For though the number of things a person can hold in his hands is limited, the number he can grasp with words is almost unlimited.

It is very important that we help our children expand their horizons through increased word knowledge. I remember when my world began opening up through the magic, the imagery of words. A schoolteacher aunt who lived with us taught me to play a game she called "String-a-Word." She would say a word such as "snow." I was to respond with the first word it made me think of. Example: "cold." She might then say "ice cream," to which I would respond "chocolate." This fun game can be played for any length of time with all ages of children from preschool to senior citizens.

Words are so important that it takes time to learn how to choose precisely the ones that express what you mean to say. In fact, word choice is an art, and you may need to spend some time developing this attribute in yourself.

There are numerous ways to teach children to use words. My first baby had a "What-Is-It?" box by the time he was able to sit up. At first the box was filled with very simple items: comb, brush, beads, spoon. As he grew older, the objects became more varied: rubber bands, thimble, and paper clips. As Terry moved each object from box to lid and back again, I would speak the object's name. I encouraged him to touch and hold each one, an important part of the game. It wasn't long before the child did the naming and I did the praising.

When this game began to grow old because it was no longer a challenge, I would put objects into a sack and allow him to reach inside and feel each one until he could identify it. As Terry and each succeeding child became more adept, I added more articles to the sack. Sometimes I put a time limit on how long the child could feel before naming as many as possible. A variation of the game was for one child to put his hand in the sack and describe an object until the others could guess what he was feeling.

Trish, when three, once described a piece of cotton to her brother with, "It's soft (a pause) . . . warm, too . . . (a longer pause). You know, squashy-warm like a lamb!" This game develops speaking and self-expression capabilities as well as helping tiny fingers to become more sensitive.

The "What-Is-It?" game, which could be considered a concrete version of "Password," is one that older children, and even adults, can find challenging. Actually, it is sometimes very difficult to describe something without actually telling what it is.

A record player or tape recorder can be a source of enrichment if the records or tapes are chosen with care. Even tiny children may be given what might be considered adult records. I have learned that very young children enjoy classical music and will listen to an Italian opera that their parents might not care for at all. I call experiences such as this mind-stretchers. Many times after playing such a record with difficult words, you will hear your child repeating the words over and over again, as though he enjoyed the sound of them or the feel of his tongue making them.

I recall the tremendous popularity of the song "Super-cali-fragil-istic-expi-ali-docius" that was a part of the Mary Poppins movie. Children of all ages enjoy onomatopoeia, which is a way of naming things according to the sound they make. For example, "The dog's tongue laps steadily at the water, slosh, slosh." The more you and your child use these kinds of words, the more he will become graphic in his conversation with others.

When I was teaching a semester of creative writing to a ninth grade class, I asked each student to choose a word that the whole class would then learn. We took only a few words at a time and put them on the blackboard. Each student learned the words and the definitions and used them in a sentence. I was amazed at the pride each student took in searching out these special words and teaching them to the class.

Because my students seemed to enjoy the exercise so much, I tried it at home, where it quickly became a favorite. Each child enjoyed the status of teaching the whole family a new word. The opportunity made him feel important; it was his word everyone was using. Even your preschooler can join in by choosing a word from his own dictionary to share.

NUMBERS

Learning to count may be introduced somewhere between the ages of one and two—not just the abstract counting of numbers in succession, but of objects. We started counting the same way we used letters, one at a time. One spoon, one bowl, one cup. A week or two later, it was two spoons, two bowls, two cups. When this was learned, we mixed two objects. Then I would say, "You have two dishes on your tray, one cup and one bowl. Let's count them: two dishes. One . . . two."

Incidentally, this will also teach adding with little effort. Learning fractions by means of cut-up circles is another absorbing game. We cut several circles the same size and colored each one differently. Then I cut one in halves, another in quarters, others in eighths and even sixteenths. This practice was a special help to our children when they took piano lessons. They needed to know the time value of the notes long before they learned fractions at school.

As the children progressed in school, I added fun math

games. One is our "Frog Game" that helped them with their multiplication. To play the game you must first learn this sentence:

One frog, two eyes, four legs, in a pond, ker-plunk, ker-plunk, ker-plunk.

Then one child or person says, "One frog." The next child says, "Two eyes." The third, "Four legs." The next says, "In a pond." The next, "Ker-plunk." The next says, "Ker-plunk." The next, "Ker-plunk."

Then we begin over with the next person saying, "Two frogs." The next person, "Four eyes." The next, "Eight legs." The next, "In a pond." The next, "In a pond." The next, "Ker-plunk." The next, "Ker-plunk." The next, "Ker-plunk." The next, "Ker-plunk." Then, "Ker-plunk." And, "Ker-plunk."

Remember, you need *one* "in a pond" and *three* "ker-plunks" for every frog. By playing this game your child will learn to multiply by two for the eyes, by four for the legs, and by three for the ker-plunks.

Another multiplication game we played was, "Buzz-Fizz." To play, you take turns counting up to fifty as fast as you can, but instead of saying *five* or any multiple of five, call out "buzz." Instead of saying *seven* or any multiple of seven, call out "fizz." One person can do this alone with another person listening to catch him making a mistake, or you can take turns and go around in the family group. If the number is a multiple of five and seven, then you must say, "buzz-fizz." Anyone who makes a mistake has to start again at one.

A game we called "Math Alert" is a utilization of all the math skills a child has accumulated. Example, the leader may say, "Four times two, add one, divide by three, take away two, times four, divide by two. What's the answer?" Each succeeding turn can become increasingly complex in order to continually challenge.

GEOGRAPHY

Some important visual challenges come from maps and a globe. Maps of your country, our world, Bible maps of

Old and New Testament kingdoms . . . and of your own
child's world.

For the very young child, the most important locations
on a map are: the place where his own house is, where
Grandma lives, or where you went on your vacation. You
can satisfy some of his basic curiosity about maps by
drawing a simple one of your neighborhood, then locating
on it the grocery store, the homes of all his friends, and
even the path across the field.

Geography started for our preschoolers at snack time.
We cut up a large map of the United States state by
state. Every other day one of the states would be laid in
the middle of the table. The kitchen was filled with
laughter as we tried to bite our crackers and toast into the
shape of whatever state had been chosen. I have seen
teenagers become quite adept at this.

For most useful results, hang maps at eye level
in an area where the family frequently gathers. We
"wall-papered" our kitchen eating area with maps. Then
when a location would come up during a conversation,
it was convenient for us to look it up while it was still fresh.
Bible stories, too, are better understood and longer
remembered if maps are visible during the storytime.

MONEY VALUE

The value of different pieces of money is important for
every child to know before handling even such small
amounts as lunch money. Each of my children received an
allowance no later than the age of three. Along with
his money he was given an allowance plate (a paper plate
with dividers to make three sections). Money was placed
in each section on Saturday. One section was for Sunday
school money; another for money to put into his bank.
(A child's bank should be one that allows him to see the
money as it accumulates.) The third section was to be
used as the child chose. He could take it to Sunday school,
put it in his bank, or buy something at the store.

Money games can be improvised by using a box full of
small change. One of our favorite money games was
our "Grocery Store" in the basement, which consisted of a

collection of empty food boxes and cans. Each was "priced" with small amounts of money and could be "purchased" from the box of change: nickels, dimes, quarters, half-dollars. Some items came to over a dollar, of course. This game taught the children both how to handle money and to count it correctly. It also helped teach appropriate ways for customers and clerks to interact with each other. This game early gave my children the poise and self-confidence they needed to become good shoppers.

TIME RESPONSIBILITY

Time means nothing to a child until he learns to "tell time." For teaching this, it is best to use both kinds of present-day clocks: digital and numeral. Also helpful are clocks with Roman numerals and those with dots instead of numerals. Learning all of these kinds of clock faces will enable a child to avoid confusion when telling time away from home.

As early as possible, a child should be given an inexpensive watch; this may be a means of helping him become responsible for being on time. Possessing his own watch helps build a child's self-respect and self-confidence, which come naturally as he learns to accept responsibility. The emotional problems many adults struggle with are the result of refusing to become responsible for their own actions. Therefore we do our children a great service when we teach them how to become responsible. Some children are continually deprived of responsibility and thus acquire a negative self-image. Such children may eventually become overly dependent adults.

GOOD MANNERS

Good manners are a part of one's personality and reveal a child's training or lack of it. The list is long and varied on the subject: eating, speaking, fairness, sharing, interrupting, tardiness. These are just a few manners a

child should learn. My personal definition of good
manners can be stated as respect for the person and
feelings of others.

To help our children become familiar with etiquette
situations they might encounter, we played "Polite
Games." For example, one would have to do with passing
through a doorway in which someone is standing. I
would explain to the child how he should conduct himself,
then stand in the doorway. The child would stop beside
me and say, "Please excuse me," or, "May I please go
through?" When I stepped aside, he would say, "Thank
you."

This is a small thing, but each small courtesy indicates
consideration for another person. A child's attitude
toward courtesy depends upon how courteous you are to
him. Since children are natural mimics, they will act like
you, in spite of your every attempt to "teach them"
good manners.

Playing "Polite Games" is a good way to teach your
child how to handle himself in numerous situations. These
games can also be used to correct a child without causing
him loss of self-respect. For example, one of my daughters
developed the habit of constantly rushing into a room
where people were conversing, and immediately breaking
into the conversation. My natural impulse was to say,
"You're interrupting!" and tell her to be quiet.

But I realize such a response could destroy an especially
exciting moment in a child's life which could never again
be shared in quite the same way. To help my daughter
overcome her annoying habit, the children and I
frequently practiced the polite game we called, "Non-
Interruption." Playing this game enabled me to
demonstrate various ways for the child to enter a room
and discreetly obtain permission to make his needs
known.

Have you ever watched a young child step on toes,
shove past knees, and knock purses over in his attempt
to reach his mother at the end of a church pew? To
correct his behavior, try lining up siblings or stuffed
animals on your couch and show your child how to pause

at each one to say, "Excuse me, please," then wait for them to move their feet or belongings before passing by.

No matter what particular difficulty you may be experiencing with your child, it can be overcome if you take the time to show him the appropriate behavior. Polite games are very effective. Children want to be respected. Children want to do what is right. And *children want the confidence of knowing how to behave.* Games such as these produce that confidence.

Learning telephone manners is especially needful in today's world. And since most callers do not appreciate the chatter of a young child who is allowed to answer the telephone before he is properly taught, I began teaching my children early. One method I employed was the "Telephone Manners Game." To play this game you need either a toy telephone, complete with dial, or an unplugged real telephone.

Show and tell your children how to answer the telephone. Then practice with them until they know exactly how to handle calls and take messages. Children should properly respond to calls by giving the residence name, followed by their own first name. As in the example that follows, this enables the caller to know immediately to whom he is speaking:

"Smith's residence. Mary speaking."

"Is your mother there, Mary?"

"Who may I say is calling, please?"

"This is Thelma."

"Yes, Thelma. One moment, please." Or, "No, ma'am, I'll get my grandmother."

One telephone house rule I found beneficial had to do with controlling the noise level when the telephone was being used. Realizing the irritation a listener experiences when he must strain to hear the caller above loud background sounds, I required all radios, phonographs, and loud discussions to be turned down or discontinued when someone was on the phone. Even a baby can learn to stop crying when the phone rings.

Equally important with receiving calls is the act of originating calls. Along with making regular outside calls,

the child should learn how to report emergencies. I had
this in mind as well as normal courtesy when I taught
my children to immediately identify themselves when
calling someone. For instance:

"Hello."

"Hello. This is Mary Smith. May I please speak to
Pam?"

Before making long distance calls to a grandparent or
anyone else who will want to speak to your child, consider
preliminary practice. Pretend you are the one who will
receive the call and let your child tell you what he wants to
say. Instead of smothering spontaneity, as some suppose,
this before-calling practice will help eliminate the all-too-
frequent telephone "freezes."

In this day of the ever-so-convenient telephone, writing
"thank you" notes is becoming a lost art. And though
writing notes of appreciation takes more time, such notes
are more appropriate for certain occasions because they
convey your thanks in a more lasting way.

How old must one be before writing a thank-you note?
Just as soon as a child begins drawing with pencil
and paper, he can start "writing" and sending notes. At
our house we will often send a thank-you note for a
kindness shown or a gift received. For instance, when a
neighbor came over and read stories, that act would be
worthy of a thank-you card.

At first the child will be able only to draw the object
or behavior for which he is saying thank you. Later he
can add the words. Naturally, these early efforts should
not provoke an English lesson or a lecture on neatness.
There is joy in spontaneity. Thank-you notes should
always be written while the enthusiasm is still bubbling,
for, as with carbonated beverages, something is lost
with the passing of time.

Something every mother should take time to learn is an
awareness of what "normal" behavioral development is
and that there is a wide range of difference within the
norm. (Your librarian can also refer you to additional
appropriate material.) Such knowledge can help alleviate
fears new mothers sometimes develop, and help you

abstain from pushing your child beyond the success limits of his maturation. One child may cut out paper dolls in a precise manner at age four, while a neighboring child cannot, but instead can easily balance a two-wheel bicycle. Both are behaviorally "normal."

I cannot emphasize too strongly that the basis of early learning to learn is for you to make it pleasant. Be friendly and relaxed with your child. Show him by your attitude that you are enjoying being with him, doing just what you're doing. Talk to him in a cheerful, enthusiastic manner and he will spontaneously join you in your fun. He will do this as long as you continuously give him the positive reinforcement of praise and physical affection he needs.

Always remember that for the game of learning to succeed, both you and your child must approach it joyously; for learning is a reward, not a punishment. Learning is the greatest adventure of life. Learning is desirable, vital, unavoidable, and, above all: life's greatest and most stimulating game.

Your child already believes this, and will always believe this, if you remember to keep him the *subject* of the learning process and not the *object* of a teaching process.

Teaching a child "to learn how to learn" has not been tried and found wanting. It has been found "time-consuming" and left untried.

TWO
CREATING THE OBEDIENCE HABIT

To insure instilling the habit of obedience in toddlers,
you must be prepared to back up each of your commands
with the same urgency you would exert if it were a case of
life or death. For the sake of the child's future well-being,
you must never allow a single command of yours to
go unheeded without immediate positive correction.

Young children have a very short attention span, and
they must learn to respond to your commands
immediately. For this reason you should never give your
toddler an order unless you expect—and receive—
immediate obedience. A child who early learns instant
obedience in small things seldom disobeys in larger things.
Never leave your child with the slightest impression
that you will accept anything less than complete
obedience.

Training in obedience should begin as soon as the child
reaches for things. Best results can be obtained by
using a positive approach. For example, when your baby
reaches for one of your breakables, say—kindly but
firmly—"No, you may not have this. Let's play with the
pretty blue ball." Then proceed to help the child follow
your suggestion. Don't wait until the child obeys before
showing your pleasure. Instead, begin your praise as soon
as the child shows signs of beginning to obey with
something like, "That's right, what a good girl!"

Such a friendly attitude on your part will influence your child to obey for two reasons: first, because he wants to please you, and second, because he likes being noticed. Usually when a very young child exhibits inappropriate behavior it's because he believes that it is the only way he can receive the attention he craves.

Many mothers talk too much or raise their voices when dealing with the negative behavior of their children. Yelling at your "kids" is like trying to drive the car by honking the horn. It doesn't work! Besides, it confuses them, as do such threats as, "If you do that I won't take you to the park anymore." Other negative verbal tools often used to discipline children are such statements as:

"You are always breaking something" (degrading).
"If you would only act like Billy" (comparing).
"The police are going to get you," or "God sees you, and he is going to punish you" (blackmailing).
"You're stupid," "You're clumsy," "You're bad" (labeling).

Never, but never call your child bad. Labels attached to preschool children, if they are internalized, will result in behavior that conforms to what the child is being told he is.

When possible don't give your child a command if you can use a request. Never ask a question if there are no options. Don't ask, for instance, "Would you like to eat lunch now?" Ask instead, "Do you prefer carrots or peas for lunch?" Never give a negative command when you can make it a positive suggestion. Instead of, "Don't walk through the puddle," say, "Let's tiptoe around the edge of the water."

CRITICIZE CONSTRUCTIVELY

It is important not only to avoid giving unnecessary commands but also to avoid unnecessary criticism. When criticism becomes necessary, it should always be constructive. Helpful criticism does not address itself to a person but deals with the event.

For example, suppose your little girl has been painting for twenty minutes and then gets some paint on the table. A quick response might be, "How many times have I told you to be careful with the paint? But you still spill it every time." But how much better to say, "You've done really well today. Even though you've been painting for a long time, you didn't spill anything until now. We'll just clean this up quickly. The next time you paint, I bet you will be able to do it without spilling a drop." Criticism—when used—should always leave the child feeling he has been helped.

PRAISE ABUNDANTLY

Most of the time when corrections are in order, it is possible to include praise. For example, speaking to a child concerning this situation: "You emptied four waste-baskets. That's good. Here's one in the bathroom. I know you wanted to empty them all by yourself." Such a comment appeals to a child's pride and sense of importance. It also avoids the opportunity for argument that could be engendered by, "You forgot to empty the bathroom wastebasket. Go get it now."

Praise your child for even the slightest movement toward obedience, no matter how minute. A case in point could be when you have said something like, "Johnny, let's pick up the toys," and the child picks up a book and opens it. His obedient momentum can be furthered with, "That's a good idea, to put away all your books first. Thank you for thinking of that."

Praise your child for his eagerness to improve himself. Even when he tries to please you by doing something that you usually do for him. A time when I was visiting in another home, a young child appeared from his bedroom, obviously very proud of himself. "Look, Mommie," he said, "I got dressed all by myself." We both looked at the child. Though he had his pants on backwards, she only praised his positive attempt to do something for himself.

"That's wonderful, Billy," she said. "That was smart of you to learn to dress yourself. I am very pleased."

The child's desire to try was bolstered by his mother's praise. And since the boy was not appearing in public with his pants on backwards, absolutely no harm was done.

GIVE RESPECT TO GAIN RESPECT

From infancy every child's right to personal privacy should be respected. A child needs unattended time when he can mull over a toy, feel it, taste it, watch the light play on it, and hide it away in his private place. Every child should have some cubicle which is his alone where he can store his personal things.

When my children were small I happened to have a lot of kitchen drawers, so each child was given one as his own. From the time the child learned to crawl to the kitchen, he quickly appropriated that drawer, which he could pull open and fill with his personal belongings. I never bothered those drawers. I never opened one without the owner's permission. And since, by word and action, I demonstrated my respect for their personal belongings, it was easier for them to respect the belongings of others.

Treating your child's valuables with respect is a healthy way to teach him how to respect the rights, privileges, and property of another. Though there are many ways to demonstrate such respect, we employed a somewhat unique one. Each week we would display one family member's valuable possessions on our living room coffee table. And whatever the object—whether a caterpillar cocoon, a paper doll family, or one of my prized cut-glass figurines—the same principle always applied: admire, but don't touch.

A fringe benefit from this project became evident when I would take the children into other homes in the community. Both the children and I were relaxed when we observed lovely items on display, for we knew that the objects were there simply to look at.

Another means of showing your respect for your child's person is to always discipline or punish in private.

Correcting your child in front of others causes embarrassment and resentment. If correction is needed and others are present, simply remove the child from the room in the most inobtrusive manner possible.

God's Word instructs us not to make it difficult for our children to obey (Eph. 6:4, Phillips).

SIBLING RIVALRY

Rivalry is bound to occur in a family of more than one child. And when it occurs, it cannot be ignored. Here is one positive way to handle sibling arguments or fights. Seat the children in a circle—this will work if there are as few as two. Have each child take a turn stating his perception of the disagreement. Then have him say something he likes about each of the others in the circle.

For instance, it's Charles' turn. He says, "I think Betty took Helen's doll away from her without asking. Helen was playing with it and wanted it back, but Betty wouldn't give it back. Then they started to fight."

Next, allow Betty and Helen to state what they think happened.

Then it will be Charles' turn again. He says: "I really like Betty. She always shares her lemonade when I ask her. Helen helps me with my race track, and that's what I like about her."

You might want to go around the circle four or five times. This practice accomplishes several things: First, it allows for anger ventilation. Second, it usually clears the air concerning the disagreement. Third, it enhances each child's self-esteem to hear the positive things his siblings think about him. Fourth, negative feelings are dissipated.

DEVELOPING PATIENCE

Patience—the marvelous gift we all desire—right now! One method we can use to help children develop this trait is rope tying. Simply tie a knot in a short length of rope and let the child untie it. Now some of you may not know any more about rope tying than I did. But I found a number of books in the library on the subject and learned several knots from them. If you are fortunate enough to know someone who has been in the Navy, he could teach you the knack. As your child learns how to untie (and eventually to tie) some of the simple knots, you can improve both his patience and ingenuity by providing him progressively more difficult and complex knots to work with.

There are also numerous children's games on the market which your child can work on quietly by himself. Puzzles are in that category. However, never give a child anything to play with that is so difficult that his ultimate success will be thwarted. This is essential. Every child (as well as every adult) has to meet with a certain degree of success if he is to continue to try.

Have you ever heard the maxim, "Success breeds success"? I'd like to coin another one: "Success also breeds patience." Provide your child with a game or puzzle he can operate or solve rather quickly. Then give him one a trifle more difficult. As he progresses in his problem-solving (puzzle-solving in this case) ability, give him even more difficult puzzles, ones that may take several hours of patient effort to solve.

By the time he has reached this point, he will be willing to put in the necessary time and effort on the project because he has learned to be confident that he will succeed.

SELF-CONTROL

Many children never learn how to be quiet. I taught my children this most treasured discipline with a game. We called it our "Quiet Game." The rules varied, but one item never changed. When I said, "Quaker," everybody would then refrain from talking and making noise, trying to see who could do so for the longest time. Sometimes sitting still would be one of the requirements. Another time one might do anything he cared to do as long as he remained quiet.

Everybody gained benefits from the "Quiet Game." As a mother I sometimes needed a time of quiet, which would be forthcoming when I said the magic word. My children learned how to amuse themselves quietly, which was appreciated by all. It was a genuine pleasure for me, their mother, to be confident that they could be quietly unobtrusive when necessary. I believe that children who have never learned the discipline of being silent will often misbehave in public because of their embarrassment at the discomfort of forced silence.

Another way to teach self-control is by pleasure postponement. When you return from the library with your child, each of you with an armload of books, you might say something like this:

"It's about thirty minutes till lunch time. Now let's talk about what you want to do."

"What do you mean?"

"Well, remember you still have some chores to do."

"Yes, but I want to look at my books now."

"I'll give you two choices. If you'd like me to help you with your chores, we'll do them right now. Then you could spend all afternoon looking at your books. That's one choice."

"What's the other one?" he asks.

"You can look at your books now, before lunch. Then after lunch you can do your chores alone. You can do whichever you like."

Several principles are involved here. First, if the child is to learn self-imposed discipline from the situation, the choice he makes must be his alone. Second, he will learn that there is usually more than one solution to almost any situation or problem. And third, by trading immediate satisfaction for future gratification, he can usually derive even greater long-range benefits.

DISCIPLINE OF WORK

From the day your child begins to toddle, you should train him to do some chores. Not only will this eventually save you many steps, but it will give the child the satisfaction of accomplishment. It also gives him the opportunity of contributing to the maintenance of "his" household.

Sometimes mothers don't teach their young children to do various small tasks because they labor under the false impression that preschoolers are too young to help. Yet a wise mother will never do for her child what he can be taught to do for himself. It is only through the satisfaction of accomplishment that a child is challenged to try progressively more difficult tasks—and to succeed at them.

One must consider himself a part of a team before he can accept the value system of the team. I used to attach a list of chores on the refrigerator from which my children could choose the ones they wished to do. Before they were able to read, I used pictures instead of a written list. This made it possible for even a very young child to choose something he would do around the house that day.

As my children grew in comprehension and understanding, I would ask each one to choose certain chores for an entire week. Then, at the end of the week, each child chose a different task. This method prevented any child from drawing either a favorite chore or a less agreeable chore two weeks in a row. Completing chores on the "chore list" gave every child the pleasure of attaching a gold star by each one he had successfully completed. The chart then became a visible form of reinforcing positive habits.

We often combined work with play by using a game we called "Links." The game was designed to be a fun way of training children's memories. Here's how it worked: I would give several commands to my child in quick succession, beginning with such easy commands as, "Please put your truck in the toy box and bring me your ball." This command, of course, gives the child two things to do. A very young child might bring you the ball and forget the truck, or vice versa. But after a few practice sessions he will usually remember both items.

When you use this method of memory training, remember that routines facilitate learning, and even the very young child will become interested in the process. He enjoys doing it just to be doing. Soon you can gradually increase the complexity and number of commands, keeping it always a game, one that stretches and trains the memory.

As the children grow older they enjoy seeing just how many commands they can remember to do in the order in which they were given. Sometimes when my children had half a dozen tasks to accomplish during a day, they would ask me to list them in a certain order. Then they would make a game of their work by trying to accomplish everything in the order in which it was given to them.

Every time you can make work a pleasure, you are strengthening positive attitudes. Work should never be used as punishment. The exception to this principle is the work caused when a child spills or breaks something or carelessly tracks in on a clean floor. We should strive to instill in our children that honest work is a privilege.

PUNISHMENT

Much of the time punishment achieves only one aim: it tells the child what he's not supposed to do. But it often fails in another respect: it doesn't tell the child what he should be doing in place of the unacceptable behavior. This will leave a child confused and angry. It must seem to some children that the only acceptable behavior is to do nothing, to be completely inactive. The child needs to be helped to find ways of responding which are satisfactory, both to himself and to his family.

Always make the punishment "fit the crime." Don't take away meaningful pleasures that have been anticipated. Example: If you plan to go to the zoo on Friday, don't cancel the trip because of a Tuesday night misdemeanor. This is unfair because it puts the child under the strain of basing his long-awaited trip on how good he is, or whether he is even good enough.

Be sure punishment does not involve innocent persons.

For instance, if your child is disobedient the same day Grandma is coming to take him for ice cream, don't withdraw that outing. Punishing the child in that manner also inflicts punishment on Grandma.

Neither should a child's full allowance be withdrawn because of his behavior. However, a neighboring family designed a positive discipline for rewarding their children with a type of allowance. They awarded each child with a coupon when he completed an assigned task and withdrew one when the child misbehaved. These coupons could be redeemed at any time for prizes. The parents made a chart displaying pictures of the various prizes available, along with the coupon "price" for each of them. These parents found this method helpful in both developing positive habits and eliminating some inappropriate behavior.

All children want to belong and will do whatever seems to be effective to achieve acceptance. As long as the child feels a sense of belonging and is not discouraged, he will respond in a positive manner to the demands and needs of the situation. It is only when he does not believe he can find his place through acceptable means and becomes discouraged that he will misbehave. God reinforces this principle by telling us, "Don't scold your children so much that they become discouraged and quit trying" (Col. 3:21, TLB).

INTERNAL DISCIPLINE

So far we have been discussing methods of external discipline, which have to do with imposed rules. But consideration should also be given to internal discipline, which has more to do with reason and conscience. This discipline doesn't depend so much on rules as on the values which inspire them.

An experiment using internal discipline was conducted by Elliot Aronson and J. Merrill Carlsmith at the Harvard University Nursery. They studied the effect of severity of threat on forbidden behavior. For ethical reasons they did not try to change basic values such as aggression.

They chose instead a trivial aspect of behavior: toy preference.

They asked five-year-old children to rate the attractiveness of several toys. Then the psychologists chose the toys that the children considered to be most attractive and told them they could not play with them. They threatened half of the children with mild punishment for transgression: "We would be a little angry if you played with it." They threatened the other half with severe punishment: "We would be very angry ... we would have to take all the toys, go home, and never come back again. We would think you were just babies."

After that they left the room and allowed the children to play with other toys and to resist the temptation of playing with the forbidden ones. All children resisted the temptation; none played with the forbidden toys.

On returning to the room, the psychologists remeasured the attractiveness of all the toys. The results were both striking and exciting. Those children who underwent the mild threat now felt the forbidden toys less attractive than before. In short, lacking adequate external justification for refraining from playing with the forbidden toys, the children succeeded in convincing themselves that they had not played with those toys because they did not really like them.

On the other hand, the forbidden toys did not become less attractive for those who were severely threatened. Those children continued to rate the forbidden toys as highly desirable. Indeed, some even found the toys more desirable than they had before the threat. The children in the severe threat condition had good external reasons for not playing with the toys. They, therefore, had no need to find additional reasons and consequently continued to like the toys.

The conclusions that can be drawn from this experiment may well apply to more important areas than mere toy preference—such as the basic principle behind successful aggression control.

Let me give a practical application. Sometimes it's

difficult to persuade larger children that it is not right or proper behavior to beat up on smaller children. Therefore, the secret is to get the children to persuade themselves that such behavior is not enjoyable. For example, your five-year-old child enjoys beating up on his three-year-old brother, and your reasoning with him has not produced adequate restraint, so you now have decided to punish the older child for his aggressiveness. You have at your disposal a variety of punishments that range from mild (a stern look) to extremely severe (a hard spanking, plus having to stand in the corner for two hours). From the above experiment we can assume that the more severe your threat, the more likely your child is to mend his ways while you are watching him—though he will probably hit his brother or others when you are not around.

Regardless of whether the punishment is severe or mild, the child will experience dissonance. Though he is now not beating up his little brother, he would like to. So when your child has the urge to hit his brother and doesn't, he, in effect, asks himself, "Why don't I?"

Under your severe threat, he has already answered himself in the form of external justification, "I don't beat up my brother, because if I do, my mother is going to spank me and stand me in the corner." That means the severe threat has provided the child ample external justification for not hitting his brother while he is being watched.

However, when the child in the mild threat situation asks himself, "How come I'm not beating up my little brother?" he doesn't have a good externally imposed reason. Because the threat from his mother was so mild, it does not provide a total justification for his nonaggression. This means that your child is now not doing something that he would like to do, and lacks sufficient external justification for not doing it.

Therefore, in this situation the child continues to experience dissonance. Since he is unable to reduce the dissonance simply by blaming his nonaggressive action on a severe threat, the child must find a way to justify to himself the fact that he is not hitting his brother. Almost invariably the best answer he can come up with is that he really does not like to beat up his brother. He then tries to convince himself that he didn't want to do it in the first place, and that beating up little kids is not fun. When you allow your child the opportunity to construct his own internal justification, you have taken a long step toward helping him develop a permanent set of values.

VALUE OF CONSISTENCY

In order to be effective in any of the preceding suggestions in this chapter, you must be consistent. The value of consistency in discipline cannot be stressed too much. It is essential that your child knows exactly what you expect of him, including the knowledge that you will always carry out any promised correction if he disobeys.

A good rule to follow if you desire to avoid inconsistency is never to forbid your child to do anything unless you mean what you say and then follow through. Make certain your child has a clear understanding of your rules. Discuss them with him in a pleasant, positive manner. Both by your manner and your attitude, your child will know that you mean what you say and that you are very capable of handling any situation.

In order to be secure, every child needs to know what his limits are. Therefore, when mothers are not consistent with their rules, they not only become the cause of their child's disobedience but also of his insecurity. A consistent mother creates a predictable environment, thus producing a comfortable climate within which her child will naturally want to be cooperative, for he feels both accepted and secure.

THREE
THE IMPORTANCE
OF PHYSICAL APPEARANCE

Obedience, of course, is not the end of authority. It is
the effect of authority. Authority does not cause
obedience; it attracts it. Authority is founded upon moral
prestige and value. It is moral force and is always
attached to a person. When the one who represents
authority—in this case, the parent—is not respected, the
inevitable result is either tyranny on the part of the
parent or license on the part of the child.

The privilege of being able to respect, to be proud of
both his parents and his home should be the right of
every child. Perhaps the greatest influence a child can
ever receive comes from his mother. If she is certain
of her position in the home and is comfortable with her
own self as a person, she will never have to exercise
extreme demonstrations of authority. For the greatest
authority a mother can demonstrate to her child is the
example of her mastery of her own self.

Paul says in 1 Corinthians 9:25, 27, "And every man
that striveth for the mastery is temperate in all things. . . .
But I keep under my body, and bring it into subjection:
lest that by any means, when I have preached to others,
I myself should be a castaway [be unapproved]." In
other words, it is my responsibility as a mother to
master myself, thereby giving my children opportunity to

"hear" my teachings through both my words and my actions.

GOD'S TEMPLES

"Know ye not that ye are the temple of God, and that the Spirit of God dwelleth in you? If any man defile the temple of God, him shall God destroy; for the temple of God is holy, which temple ye are" (1 Cor. 3:16, 17). Most of us become quite concerned about the appearance of the church building where we worship: unkempt pews, unwashed windows, and unmowed lawns. Important as it is to care for the church building, God's Word indicates that we should be even more careful of our own physical appearance.

Whether we like it or not, our appearance tells other people something about how we see ourselves. This is especially true of our children who see us in private. In the light of the above Scripture passage, if I really believed that my body is the temple of God Almighty, would I habitually allow my children to see me in a soiled robe or torn, unironed dress? Would I beautify my hair and face only for the public? Would my child be embarrassed to bring his friends into his home at any time to meet his mother? Would he prefer that his mother not become a part of his Sunday school parties and school trips?

One of the most rewarding compliments ever paid to me came from my oldest son when he was twelve years old. One day he came home from school and invited me to go with his class to see a space show.

"Only one mother from our class was invited," he explained. "When the teacher asked who wanted his or her mother to go, I raised my hand. Only two other kids raised their hands. Then all the kids voted on which mother they wanted, and you won. Probably because they know you best." (I had been the homeroom mother for several years.) "Anyway," he continued, "it's the first time I've ever been able to volunteer you for something that I thought would be especially interesting to you."

A lump rose in my throat as I looked at my eldest

son who was fast approaching his teen years. He's going on an all-day trip and wants me to go, I thought.
He still enjoys himself in my presence and wants to share this special event with me.

Terry was looking hard at me. "Aren't you going to say something? I thought you would be glad."

I swallowed. "I am glad. Thank you for asking me. Of course, I'll go."

At that moment I realized how privileged a mother is whose child views her with pride. Today I realize *how privileged a child is whose mother gives him the opportunity to view her with pride.*

All too often we mothers allow ourselves to become so busy with our family that we don't think about being responsible for our appearance. We tell ourselves that we are sacrificing for the children, when in reality we are cheating them. Every child is like a mirror in the sense that he reflects the influences around him and transfers them into his own nature. So if your behavior does not reflect a belief that your body is the temple of God, you will never convince your child that his is.

YOUR CLOTHES ARE TALKING

Whatever you wear makes a statement of some kind. Every time you dress, you make choices about the way you want to appear, and even an "I-don't-care" message is a clear statement. Your clothing affects your own mood as well as that of your child. Suppose one afternoon you and your child decide to paint a picture. If both of you are wearing crisp, clean shirts your painting will reflect a different mood than if you are both still dragging around in pajamas.

Even the kind of clothing we wear is important and influences our posture and movement. It serves either to animate or slow us down. Society is aware of this principle and uses clothing to help enforce its rules. Thus the dress codes of restaurants, schools, etc., are intended to control behavior as much as to control appearance.

A case in point: Once when I was serving as a member

on a public school board, we experimented with a
stricter, more formal dress code. At first only the teachers
participated and the discipline problems decreased to
a slight degree. Then we imposed a mandatory dress code
for students and discipline problems decreased
dramatically.

I discovered that this principle also worked at home.
When my daily appearance began to improve, the
children's behavior also improved. And when I paid closer
attention to both the kind and condition of the clothing
they wore (which generally made little difference in
the cost factor), they voluntarily took a greater interest
in their own appearance. Result: immediate positive
behavioral improvement.

Some mothers may feel that too much emphasis is being
placed on clothing and appearance in this chapter.
Remember, the manner in which you as a mother choose
to dress usually accents a certain aspect of your
personality. This is true of anyone. Often, as in the case of
a child, the trait becomes heightened until he finally
becomes that which he most strongly projects.

"What Do My Clothes Say?" is a personal appearance
game that children from three to four like to play.
To play, you simply point at an article of clothing and ask
a question.

For example: It is my turn. I point to my freshly
starched white blouse and ask my three-year-old son,
"What does my blouse say?" I think it is telling him
I want to look fresh and nice for him.

He answers, "It says, 'Don't hug me.' "

I point to his shirt that is wrong-side out and backwards.
"Your shirt tells me you were in a hurry to get dressed,
so you were careless."

"No, Mother," he says, "it's supposed to tell you that
I'm a ballplayer, and this (pointing to the label, size 6)
is my number."

The game will show both you and your child that other
people don't always see us the way we intend them to.
And as your child grows older this concept will help
him understand that the way people act toward him is

affected by the way he dresses himself. When learned early this insight can ease some strained mother-child relationships that often arise over clothing and hairstyle conflicts.

Many polls register the fact that hairstyle is one of the most frequent points of contention between teenagers and parents. Much of this can be avoided if you begin early to allow a child to express himself by choosing several hairstyles.

When you take your child visiting, and when he begins school, give him the option as frequently as possible to wear his hair in whatever manner he chooses. Then play the same game about hair that you did about clothes. You may be surprised what he thinks of your hairstyle.

If you develop this kind of open dialog from preschool years on, by the time your child is a teenager you'll be able to say: "The hairstyle covering your eyes that you wore yesterday conveys to me the idea that you want to be private. Therefore, since we are going shopping together, would you please wear your hair back, so I will feel more able to share with you?"

Because your child has played this game through the years, such a request will not threaten his personal identity, and a heated debate will not ensue.

WHERE IT BEGINS

A positive physical appearance begins with good nutrition. Several excellent books which can help you understand the value of proper nutrition are: *Everything You Always Wanted to Know About Nutrition,* by David Reuben, M.D. (Simon & Shuster); *Encyclopedia of Fruits, Vegetables, Nuts, and Seeds for Healthful Living,* by Joseph M. Kadans, Ph.D. (Parker Publishing Company); *How to Eat Right and Feel Great* and *The Total Health Cookbook,* by Virginia Rohrer (Tyndale House Publishers).

Mothers who understand the importance of good nutrition also realize that eating a properly balanced diet with little or no junk food can greatly influence their child's energy level and learning ability. And—important to every adolescent—the elimination of highly sugared foods and beverages will also lower or limit the greatly dreaded plague of acne. As a mother you can assist in developing your child's tastes for healthful foods by preparing and presenting them in interesting, attractive ways.

It is essential that you initiate such a "creative nutrition program" as early in the child's life as possible, because it is during the child's preschool years that he acquires most of his food preferences.

For example, candy, cookies, and chips have become the standard American snacks. That means that if the child next door is munching on chocolate chip cookies or candy mints, your child may become dissatisfied with his own plain carrot or celery stick. The situation provides you with another chance to use your creativity. Here are a few suggestions to get you primed:

Prepare a small apple by inserting several toothpicks upon which have been impaled cheese chunks, raisins, olives, or dates. Fill a paper cup with radish fans (make thin, parallel cuts on one side of radish to about ¼ inch of other side), carrot curls (use potato peeler to cut thin strips of carrot, drop into ice water to curl), cucumber petals (run a sharp-tined fork down the length of an unpared cucumber, then cut into thin crosswise slices), broccoli buds or cauliflowerets (break or cut broccoli or cauliflower into bite-size flowerets) and radish roses (slice off root end, cut thin "petals" around radishes from root end almost to stem end).

Prepare enough of the fancy vegetables for several days, then put in ice water to crisp and curl. They will keep a week when refrigerated in water. However, the water should be changed daily.

Sometimes snacks are more fun when supplied with a fancy pick to spear them. You can find a variety of these party picks at grocery, party, or variety stores, or at card shops.

For a taste-tempting change of pace, prepare a cup of

these crispies and a cup of peanut butter (or other nutritious) dip along with party picks.

Some variations of your healthful snacks can include: a cored apple filled with unsalted nuts or trail mix (make your own using a health food recipe), or an orange to suck. Kids love this fun snack which is prepared as follows: Use a potato peeler and thinly pare the thin outside layer of skin from the top half of the orange. Use a sharp knife to cut a small, round hole in the top, saving the top as a stopper (part of the fun is having a stopper). Next, cut the membrane of each section around the inside of the orange. This allows the juice to flow freely when the child circles the hole with his mouth and squeezes the orange with both hands.

Wrap chunks of cheese with purple and green cabbage leaves and skewer with party picks for another colorful treat. Dates filled with cream cheese served in fluted candy paper are also very special.

Any of these snacks will also enhance the lunches you and your preschool children enjoy together at home. Suggestions to "interest-ify" these intimate lunches: Fill a small hollowed-out green or red pepper with chilled shrimp and pickles.

Create a rag-doll salad. My mother introduced me to this delightful creation when I was a child. She used a peach half, round side up, or a lettuce leaf for the "body" (with tuna, chicken, or egg salad beneath it), cut celery or zucchini sticks for the limbs, and dates for the feet. The head is half a hard-boiled egg, with raisins, nuts, pimientos, or peppers for its face and shredded carrots or cheese for hair.

Children also love open-faced sandwiches cut with a cookie cutter. Not only do they enjoy eating these sandwiches, they are also very creative in helping to make them. Besides being tasty, these sandwiches also provide a good way to use up the crust ends of several loaves of bread.

Every innovative minute you spend on nutritious snacks will be repaid a thousandfold as your child naturally develops lifelong nutritious eating habits.

At the same time you are shaping your child's good eating habits, you can maximize your efforts by encouraging good table manners: combing hair, tucking in shirts (even replacing soiled ones with clean ones when necessary). This is a subtle but effective way to improve table decorum.

HOW IS YOUR TABLE DRESSED?

Table manners are affected by the way the table and food are presented. Whenever you have flowers, arrange them in a container and put them on the table. Candles are always special to young children, and fun even at breakfast. A bowl or basket of fruit or vegetables is colorful. If you get stuck for ideas, borrow library books on making centerpieces.

When I was a young girl I used to look forward to eating at the home of one of my aunts. This gracious Southern lady said, "Eating together around the table should always be an event." Eating at her table was. I hardly remember what we ate, but I do remember how special the table looked.

There were always starched, snowy-white linen napkins. Personally, I don't starch my napkins, but I have learned that even in this day of paper abundance, it is more economical to use cloth napkins than paper. We have several colors and patterns, along with a selection of napkin rings, all of which add variety to our meals. Young children love napkin rings. They also delight in fancily folded napkins. And they will quickly learn how to fold napkins into hats, ties, fans, and flowers. (For an excellent instruction booklet on folding napkins, write to the Navigators Conference Office, P.O. Box 20, Colorado Springs, CO 80901, and ask to purchase their "Hostess Ideas.")

Another item on my aunt's table that engendered a lifelong habit for me was her crystal goblets. All children know that even water tastes wonderful from a crystal goblet. Attractive and inexpensive imitation crystal can be purchased at most discount stores. And when dessert is served in tall-stemmed dessert cups, it's fantastic—even if it is only applesauce. My preschool children soon learned the difference between plastic cups and crystal glasses—and preferred the latter.

I believe that table settings can be a part of the refining influence that every child needs in his life. Milk cartons and food wrappers of any kind were forbidden at my aunt's table. And by her example I became conscious of the importance of choosing the best color-coordinated dishes I had, to blend or contrast with the colors of the foods being served.

Silverware was never "put" on the table. Instead, it was carefully laid. When my own children were old enough to set the table, I brought some library books home that showed proper ways of setting the table. Young children love the confidence that comes from knowing how to do something just right, and correctly setting a table is no exception. Experience has taught me that children who develop correct table manners usually have a correct table at which to develop them.

THE NON-EATING DIET

Relentless eating makes both flesh and spirit flabby. Fasting cripples Satan's attacks on my body, which is his prey. (See 1 Pet. 5:8.) The more I deny the fleshly appetites of my body, the more I deny Satan access to my body. Therefore, yesterday I fasted again.

Fasting is not starving. Fasting does not exhaust the body's reserves. Thousands of people have fasted under medical supervision for as long as twenty-five to thirty days. And many more thousands fast at least twenty-four hours each week.

For many people, fasting is an unusual or mystical experience, often enshrouded with anxiety, apprehension, and even fear. Since one must first be divested of these fears in order to gain the most from a fast, let me suggest two very helpful books. The first is written by a medical doctor and the second by a theologian.

The two books are: *Fast Your Way to Health,* by J. Harold Smith, M.D. (Thomas Nelson Publishing, Nashville, Tenn.) and *Restoration Through Fasting,* by Derek Prince (P.O. Box 14306, Dept. B., Fort Lauderdale, Fl.).

Fasting helps remove toxins (poisons) from the body's tissues and thus allows the body to consume its excess fat. Personally, I don't have a weight problem, but I don't intend to wait until I have one to say no to food. Fasting helps remind me that my body is a divine building, a home for God's Spirit. As long as I properly observe the laws of nutrition, all of my bodily organs will be properly nourished and thus operate at optimum efficiency. But whenever I violate these divinely instituted laws, a penalty must be paid. That penalty is some form of ill health. All of this is natural. It would be presumptuous for me to expect God to bring health and healing to my body when I have refused to obey the known dietary laws.

Paul says in 1 Corinthians 6:12 (Amplified Bible), "Everything is permissible for me—allowable and lawful; but not all things are helpful—good for me to do, expedient and profitable when considered with other things. Everything is lawful for me, but I will not become the slave of anything or be brought under its power."

The issue we face in fasting is this: Shall the cravings of the physical be my master? The cries for physical satisfaction, though not wrong in themselves, must ever be servant and not master.

Fasting is self-imposed control of the appetite. Preschool children can begin learning control of their appetites by voluntarily giving up desserts or sweets on your own day of fasting.

Explain to the child your purpose in fasting. Then give him the choice of having a dessert or joining you for a job around the house during your exercise time. The choice to partake of the food or the exercise should be completely voluntary on his part. And if he chooses the exercise instead of the food, this could become the beginning of a habit that will stand him in good stead for many years.

In chapter two I also gave other suggestions for helping a child develop self-control. However, the first principle of self-control is to be provided with a model. And a child's most consistent model should be his mother. When your child enters school and you begin warning him about drug abuse and addiction, your warnings will fall on deaf ears if *all your* appetites are not under tight control.

You see, the respect that your child has for advice and rules grows naturally from the respect that he has for the person who gives them. For example, if baseball player Pete Rose were to advise your child on how to hold a bat, the child would make an immediate effort to conform to Rose's rules. That is because of the high regard, the respect the child holds for the giver of the advice. As mothers, we must always remember that there is never respect for a command unless there is respect for the commander. Thus we will never be effective in controlling our child unless we first control ourselves.

Since fasting cuts not only excess food, but also subsistence food, during my fasting days I am more acutely aware of the world's hunger—and of the more than 12,000 people who starve to death every day. All this reminds me to count my blessings and to send, not just excess dollars, but subsistence monies to a Christian famine-fighting organization.

At our house we use the World Vision "Love Loaf." This loaf-shaped bank sits in a prominent place in our kitchen—an ever-present reminder of others who do not have enough bread to eat.

In order to encourage our children in meaningful fasting and sharing, when they have gone without a meal, they are given the predetermined price of a meal to put into the Love Loaf. Or, if they gave up dessert or a snack for the same purpose, they are given the predetermined amount of money for the Love Loaf. They are also encouraged to share their allowance, gift money, or extra money they have earned. This means that it costs the child something to learn to share.

To help make their personal giving more concrete and meaningful, I read World Vision's literature describing their hunger-relief projects, then shared the information with the children. My sharing of this well-written literature helped give them a clear understanding, both of the need, and how their sacrificial giving was helping to alleviate the need.

There are other reasons, too, why I fast regularly. A very important one is because the Bible advocates fasting and gives specific instructions regarding this practice in a number of places, including Isaiah 58 and Matthew 6. Also, I have found that regular fasting tends to sharpen my mental processes. (Much of this book was written during times of fasting.)

Fasting gives my digestive system a much-needed rest. As my body becomes completely "cleaned out" during a fast, I find that I have increased energy, a keener alertness, and a brighter disposition toward life.

GRACIOUS LIVING

My writing career was launched because of this topic. I read an article in a national Christian magazine that stated unequivocally that "gracious living and children do not mix." I wrote a letter of protest to the editor. He responded by inviting me to write a rebuttal for publication in his magazine. I did, he printed it, and my writing career began.

Every Christian home ought to be a place where each person living there can do so graciously. "Practice hospitality to one another. . . . And [in each instance] do it ungrudgingly—cordially and graciously without complaining [but as representing Him]" (1 Pet. 4:9, AB). And because we represent God, we will choose to have a home of refinement.

Webster says refinement is freedom from impurities, from coarseness and vulgarity. That definition includes factors which are both tangible and intangible—intangible in attitudes and conversation; tangible in furnishings and neatness.

We can take a tip from the professional decorator. He wouldn't come into your home and immediately begin by selecting color schemes, furniture, etc., which personally appealed to him. He would first spend time getting to know your family's likes and dislikes, mode of living and, above all, your personalities.

So begin your adventure in gracious living as a professional would—on paper. (After all, you too are a professional: a professional homemaker.) Analyze yourself and those who live with you. Think of interests, hobbies, habits, work, and personalities. As you do this your home decor will begin to take shape—it will be molded by who your family is.

COLOR

Color is your most powerful decorating tool. It is also the least expensive, easiest, and quickest tool to use to change or to create a decorating scheme. If you understand color and what it can do for you, you can change the visual size and shape of a room as well as create an atmosphere, adding warmth, vitality, and beauty to your home.

The prevailing color in an environment may have important effects on the kind of communications that take place there. In general, it is believed that the "warm" colors—yellow, orange, red—stimulate creativity, making most people feel more "outgoing" and responsive to others. "Cool" colors—blue, green, gray—have a tendency to encourage meditation and deliberate thought processes and may have a dampening effect on both the level and the quality of communication. The secret to using color successfully is to have a working knowledge of the basics. Any of us can learn the techniques from library reference books and appropriate magazines.

PICTURES

Think of pictures as the easiest means of adding life, color, and sparkle to a room. Pictures will do more than any other accessory to give an area charm and distinction —since they are not only decorative in themselves, but also "open up" the bare walls of a room and provide a place for the eyes to rest.

It is not necessary that every picture be hung. Some may be used effectively to punctuate bookshelves and other areas. Several colorful and attractively framed smaller pictures placed on chests or tables can add to the individuality of a room. Hang pictures in unexpected places. If a picture is interesting and well-framed, it will add spice to a room. Pictures are meant to be enjoyed, and what better way to do this than by placing them where they can be easily viewed?

We had an upstairs hallway that we called the "children's picture gallery." On the walls were hung a variety of frames, sizes, shapes, and colors. These frames all had a common denominator in that they were easy to open and change the picture. When the children painted or brought home a school masterpiece, we chose the frame most suitable and swapped an early creation for the latest. The children were very proud of their gallery and took a greater interest in drawing and painting, knowing that their pictures weren't going to be tossed out in a day or two.

A city near where we lived had a special service available through the public library. They called it, "Painting Loans." The library had a good selection of reproductions of fine paintings which could be borrowed on one's library card for one month. We appreciated this service because it gave our family the opportunity to enjoy some paintings that we would otherwise have been unable to obtain.

FLOOR

Choosing a floor covering is sometimes viewed as a fairly perfunctory process. However, floor treatment can be and often is the focal point of a room's decoration. This is particularly true for small children who spend much of their time on the floor. You can subtly or boldly create the floor stage you want to set with carefully chosen accent or area rugs.

PLANTS

You can make any room come alive with the addition of greenery. Whether you choose foliage or flowering plants, or a combination of the two, greenery can add a perfect finishing touch to any room.

When choosing plants, be sure to consider the style or furnishings you have. Large plants with shiny leaves are ideal for contemporary rooms with slim, sleek furnishings, while other plants with lacy leaves are often more at home in traditional or country style surroundings.

Don't let the size of your house or age of your children curb your enthusiasm for greenery. Even in a small room or area, a tall plant takes up very little floor space and contributes a great deal of interest. And even a toddler will enjoy caring for *his* plants. (Note: Chapter four names some fast-growing plants that are children's favorites.)

With a minimal amount of research, effort, money, and time, your home can say to each person who lives there that *he belongs.*

The furnishings of your child's room are of special importance, for his room is an extension of himself. The colors, furniture, and accessories in it should definitely reflect the child's own preferences as soon as he is able to articulate them. Your idea of a little girl's room may be pink and white ruffles. But Mary Ellen herself may prefer brown and green African animals.

Every child should have his own bulletin board. This is especially important if he shares a room. You can begin to fill his bulletin board with brightly colored pictures while he is still in the crib. As soon as he is old enough to cut pictures out of magazines and possess his own special "treasures," it is important that you no longer choose what goes on the board. If there is a difference of opinion between what you think should be on the board and what the child likes there, the choice should be his.

Bed-making can be learned and begun at age three. If your child is always encouraged and helped, when necessary, to make his bed immediately upon arising, it will become an accepted routine before he is old enough to decide that he doesn't like it. This is also true of establishing a pattern for cleaning. There should be nothing in his room that he cannot touch. If he feels that the room is really his, he will want to bring his friends there. And it is about the time he attains school age that your child begins to establish the habit of bringing friends home or not.

Whether or not a child is proud of his home is not dependent on the size of the house or the cost of the sofa. It depends on your intangible attitude which always manifests itself in the tangible evidence of the care you give your home. And if you choose to live graciously, then your home will exclaim to your child and to all who enter, "Welcome." And even more important, *"I like it here!"*

FOUR
HOME IS A FUN PLACE TO LIVE

Children should experience their first and best good times
at home. It is during their first five years that we have
the most time to know and be with our children. Yet
these years are so often filled with confusion and just
"getting through" that the golden opportunities to have
good times together are lost. The purpose of this chapter
is simply to offer ideas of how to beneficially enjoy
these years.

How do you relate holidays to daily life?

NEW YEAR'S DAY

New Year's Day was a family day for us. On it we played
all those games, new and old, for which the children
had been begging.

It was a time of reflecting on the year gone by. As we
read together our Answered Prayers Book (see chapter
12), we would strengthen each other's faith. This
gave the children confidence to go to God for their
personal needs and desires.

VALENTINE'S DAY

In our home the dining table was always chosen as the
special place for our main decorative efforts. On

Valentine's Day, the children loved to make a large heart, covered with foil or red paper. In the center they placed a picture of Jesus. Valentine's Day offers individuals of every age opportunity for creativity. From their earliest valentine exchanges, my children always made their own. They loved to do this and unabashedly used their valentines to share both Jesus' love and theirs. One year they cut red hearts from construction paper, then folded them double. On the outside were the words, "I love you—but." On the inside: "Jesus loves you more." One of my sons' friends was quite touched when he received one of these cards. It was the first time he had ever been told that Jesus loved him.

ST. PATRICK'S DAY

Most children have difficulty understanding the Trinity. This complex Christian concept is much easier for them to understand if they can handle an object that illustrates that doctrine. On St. Patrick's Day each of our children would help me bake and then take shamrock cookies to school or Sunday school to treat his class. For several years their teachers allowed them to tell their class how St. Patrick is thought to have used the shamrock to illustrate the doctrine of the Trinity.

NEW SEASON

"How Great Thou Art" became our family theme song for the day that ushered in a new season. What a wonderful time to study nature. I wanted my children to know how God so lovingly planned our world.

And children who help plant plants never walk on flowers, but instead cut bouquets for the table (with long stems). Most preschool children can be very enthusiastic about putting seeds in the ground and watering them for a time. But even radishes grow too slowly and the children soon resent their garden duties unless you cheerfully offer your help.

Castor beans, sunflower seeds, and string beans produce

immediate, tremendous rewards for a child because of
their giant size and rapid growth. And even a narcissus
bulb that grows quickly and easily in a shallow bowl,
with only water and a few pebbles or shells, will delight your
youngster. Keep a ruler handy and help him measure
the growth each day.

We discovered that from the lowly carrot will grow a
lovely new fern. To produce this "magic," simply cut off
the carrot about one inch below the greenery. Trim
off most of the old fern and stand this trimmed carrot in a
shallow bowl with water in it. A sweet potato can be
sprouted in a glass of water by putting the narrow end into
the water supported by toothpicks. The child will
delightedly watch the roots grow first, followed soon by a
lovely vine. Place the plant in a sunny place and remind
the child to add water occasionally.

One of the best experiments I have found for showing
your children how living things complete the life
cycle is to save the pumpkin seeds from their Halloween
pumpkin. Show the child how to place the seeds in a
dry place and spread them out to prevent them from
rotting. In the spring be sure to soak the seeds overnight
before planting to help insure success. After your
child has watched the vines grow and bloom—and
observed the green pumpkins turn orange—he will be
ready to make his jack-o-lantern, then save the seeds to
start all over again.

An indoor experiment that children love is the sprouting
of grass or bird seeds on a sponge in a saucer. Place
the sponge in the sunlight and keep it very wet. Children
also love to watch the way lima beans or navy beans
will swell the first day when placed in water, then quickly
open and begin sprouting. Keep the beans on a piece of
soaked cotton to prevent them from drying out, being
careful that they are not completely submerged.

Our children always looked forward to the first day of
spring. On that day we usually decked out our dining
table with a centerpiece that shouted spring. One favorite
was a bird's nest filled with eggs on which a stuffed
mother bird was sitting. On a nearby branch we perched

the father bird. Swinging from another branch we placed a card with the words from Matthew 6:26 written upon it. As we worked together constructing our centerpiece we would talk about how God planned for families.

EASTER

Easter was always an especially joyful season. On the dining table went our "peek box." A peek box is a shoe box which has a hole (about the size of a half-dollar) cut into one of the ends. The lid has a long rectangle cut into it which is covered with thin tissue paper that will allow light to filter through. Inside the shoe box an appropriate holiday scene is created. The lid is then taped on and everyone has his turn "peeking" through the round hole.

For Easter Sunday I set up a tomb in the peek box with a large "doorway" stone nearby. The empty linen grave cloths could be seen inside the vacant tomb. Outside the tomb I placed an angel sitting on the stone. Three women were stooping to look in.

When the children were small, I always surprised them by having the peek box already prepared on Easter morning. Later the older ones enjoyed making it for their younger brother and sister. The peek box was such a favorite that we often used it for other special days, by creating an appropriate seasonal scene.

Of course Easter wasn't complete without baskets and egg hunts. Each child was given as many eggs as there were words in the Bible verse he had chosen and memorized. The younger ones would use a phrase, such as "He is risen," "Christ arose." We would print one word on each egg before it was colored. When the hidden eggs were found, they were placed in a basket on which that verse was written. Anyone finding all the eggs to complete a whole verse rated a special prize.

MAY DAY

Let's dig out the lost art of creating and delivering May Day baskets! What fun my children and I had on the

evenings before as we created the baskets our
imaginations dreamed up. Then we filled them. In the
north, since it's often difficult to find flowers by this date,
I had my children plant some early flowers for this
purpose. Of course this made the baskets even more fun to
make, to give—*and* to receive. Sometimes instead of
flowers we would fill some of the baskets with cookies cut
in flower shapes. Then, after the delight of creation,
the children also enjoyed an afternoon ringing doorbells
and sharing their joy.

HONOR THY FATHER AND THY MOTHER

"Honor thy father and thy mother that thy days may
be long upon the land which the Lord thy God giveth
thee." I believe this truth needs to be taught every
day, but on the nationally set aside days, children should
be encouraged to show their love toward their parents
and grandparents in a special way.

A friend of mine has a unique way of showing love to
her working mother. She believes that she honors her
mother (this goes for both parents) by giving of herself. So,
instead of a gift, she sends her a note promising to
supply her with some baked goods once a week for a given
time. There is double reward for those who practice
this philosophy: Their children will return their love to
their own parents as they have been taught by example.

One year one of my sons presented me with a
homemade card inside of which he had printed, "I will
take out the trash cans for a month." True, this was
often his job anyway. But I was pleased that he cheerfully
took this disliked task upon himself.

FAMILY BIRTHDAYS

Family birthdays are very important; we always
celebrated such with a cake and candles. We would
decorate the honoree's chair and have his favorite meal.
After eating, I would reflect over his life and relate
a few incidents which showed God's love and care for
him as an individual.

One mother I knew made a loose-leaf birthday notebook for each child. In it she placed pictures of the special event and wrote a little story of the day's happenings. Such a book helps reassure her children that they are special.

It's fun occasionally to have a party when it isn't somebody's birthday. Some ideas are: a *Hose Party*. For this one your child is allowed to call up a few of his friends and invite them over at a specific time to run through the hose or sprinkler. Tell the children to wear their swimsuits and bring a towel or pair of shorts. Then you provide water pistols for every one as a favor.

Another is a *Sandbox Party*. Children are invited to come for a specific amount of time to play in the sandbox. Little surprises can be hidden in the sandbox and each child instructed that he is allowed to find only one. These can be such things as magnets, a package of soap bubbles, small shovels, or other small toys.

Try a *Paper Bag Party*. Invite a few of your children's friends over for lunch. Each child brings his own lunch in a paper sack. You provide an outside picnic area where they can eat, and include a drink to be sipped through straws. A variation would be to have the children bring their own drinks in thermos bottles.

A *Cookie-Making Party* for a small number of children is fun. It's really a "cookie decorating" party, for I've learned it's better to have the dough made before the children arrive. Then allow the children to help roll it out. Each child chooses the cutters to cut the cookies for his own pan. After baking, all get to sit at the table and "decorate." For this part of the adventure I provided squirt tubes of frosting, raisins, cinnamon drops, and various other decorations. The cookies they didn't eat I let them keep and take home. To make this particular type of party successful you'll need: a table big enough to work on, enough materials to work with, and a long-suffering mother!

Dressing-Up Party. Young children love to playact and are glad to get a chance to do it with others. And Halloween costumes are as much fun in June as in October.

Consider having a *Circus Party*. Let everyone bring his favorite "wild" animal, which could include a goldfish, a turtle, a dog, or a cat. Have your backyard fixed up with tables and places to display different animals. The children can take turns going around looking at all the other "wild" animals. Of course, each child will be given opportunity to tell about his own. This party calls for lots of balloons.

JULY FOURTH

When July Fourth rolled around, I asked myself several questions, such as, "How really patriotic are we? Do my children know our national anthem? Have they learned 'God Bless America,' 'Faith of Our Fathers' and other soul-stirring hymns?"

I decided to teach them the history of the day, and made it a practice to do so on each nationally observed patriotic day.

To prepare yourself, spend some time looking up interesting facts and events so that you can present a lively story. As your children grow old enough, challenge each of them to search out new facts about the day. One family I know rewards the child who has found the most unusual fact with the honor of raising the flag.

And don't neglect to have *Band Parades*. Every mother of young children has become aware of individual musical talent among her children at very early ages, evidenced by their beating the table with silverware, tapping glasses of milk, or blowing bubbles in orange juice.

In order to channel this budding talent in a civilized fashion, here are some suggestions for instruments that are fun to use and easy to make. Staple two paper plates together facing each other, then fasten four or five jingle bells. Allow the child to color his "tambourine" with crayons. A variation is to tie the bells to an old embroidery hoop. To make a rattle, fill a baby food can with seeds, beans, rice, or whatever is handy. A used toilet paper tube can be filled the same way. After inserting the "music makers," stuff paper in both ends and use a rubber band to keep it in place.

Drill a hole in a dry gourd, fill with beans or rice
and tape the hole. And presto: a nice shaker. A horseshoe
hung by a cord and struck with a long nail serves as an
effective triangle. Cymbals can be created from two
pot lids. Tie a ribbon or yarn around the handle for a
special decorative effect. Bells sewed to a strip of elastic
are fun to wear around the wrist or ankles for special
musical effects.

Your guitar can be made from a shoe box or cigar box
around which you have stretched several rubber bands.
Children love to pluck or strum such an instrument.
Wrap a piece of waxed or tissue paper over a comb and
hum into it. Thumbtack sandpaper on blocks of wood
and swish them together at the proper place in the
"concert." (Note: This instrument's sound has been known
to cause spinal chills!)

And of course the drum. A two-pound coffee can with
both ends removed becomes the base. Cover the ends
with inner tubing rounds cut to overlap an inch or two.
Punch holes around the edges and lace up with a plastic
clothesline or heavy cord.

BIRTHDAYS OF GREAT AMERICANS

Use the birthdays of great Americans for reminding
your children of their Christian heritage. Plan a birthday
meal with cherry pie for George Washington, log cake
for Abraham Lincoln, peanut butter pie for George
Washington Carver, etc. Your child's life will be greatly
enriched when he learns to admire men of God such as
those whom all the world acknowledges.

THANKSGIVING DAY

Our Thanksgiving Days have a built-in reminder of those
less fortunate. On that day each member of our family
brings money he has saved. We combine it and send it to
the organization or individual the children decide is
most needy.

Each child has prepared himself for the day by making

a picture or poster to be hung in the dining room.
Across the top he has printed, "I'm thankful for . . ." His
sketches or clippings describe the things he's been most
grateful for that year. I show each child how to make his
own "turkey apple." These are simple and decorative.
Four toothpicks jammed with raisins are stuck across the
back of an apple. A stuffed olive on a toothpick becomes
the head and the red pimiento hanging out becomes
the wattle. Stick three toothpicks in the bottom for legs
and you have a delightful edible favor.

CHRISTMAS

Where is the person, young or old, who doesn't get a lilt
in his voice at the coming of Christmas? I always kept
my children busy making their own gifts and cards—not
just for friends and family but for someone who was shut
in or confined in the hospital. Children who are included
in the preparations for giving don't spend as much
time wondering and asking, "What am I getting?"

On Christmas Eve day our children presented a much-
practiced play for whomever happened to be there. The
evening was complete with a decorated cake, around
which the children sang "Happy Birthday" to Jesus. Each
gave a gift—as unto him—whether a hanky for the
crippled lady down the street, or a rededication of abilities
to God.

FAMILY GIFT EXCHANGE DAY

I know of a family that decided to give only to others
at Christmas, to concentrate on helping the less fortunate.
In order for their children to learn how to participate
joyfully in such a selfless Christmas atmosphere, they
chose to have a Family Gift Exchange Day every two
months throughout the year (January, March, May, July,
September, November).

Since anticipation was important, the dates were set
in advance. This gave time to talk and plan for every
special FGED. Each family member received only one

gift each time. The meal was prepared with favorite foods; everyone dressed up and a party atmosphere prevailed.

Such a plan has many advantages. Financially it is easier to spread gift spending over the year, thus taking advantage of sales, and seasonal items can be used immediately. Obviously, children have greater appreciation for a special gift several times a year than for so many all at once. And, best of all, excitement abounds throughout the year.

CALENDARS

Calendars are very important for a preschool child to be able to look ahead to these special events and others that personally affect him: Grandma's visit, dental appointment, his pet's birthday, etc. To make this possible, I hung a large calendar at child's eye level in a convenient location. I chose a calendar that had large squares for each day, large enough for us to color or draw in anticipated happenings.

With such a calendar my children then "xed" off the days as they went by, thus enabling them to begin visualizing events in relation to time. Very young children often prefer a vertical form calendar. They can more easily learn to read and utilize such a calendar if you will cut squares and print dates and events on each. Glue the squares to a long ribbon. At the end of every day your child can cut off that square and throw it away. In this manner he can visually understand the approach of a looked-forward-to event. A vertical calendar is especially enjoyed during the birthday month or prior to Christmas, Easter, or some other very special occasion.

SUPPLIES

As you can see, the projects described in this chapter require a variety of supplies. Experience has taught me that a preschool child will seldom be bored if he has sufficient quantities of many items to work with, especially if he has some assistance. A special cupboard should be set aside to stock all or some of the following items. This will enable you to select nearly anything on the spur of the moment that will give your child something to keep him happily involved.

A selection of painting smocks will be useful to provide for children who are involved in "messy" activities. These can be made from mother's blouses or dad's shirts (with sleeves cut off), worn backwards and buttoned up.

Here is a partial listing of supplies you will want to keep on hand: plain or colored toothpicks—to be used for arranging into different designs, or for poking into potatoes, cucumbers, or apples; colored pipe cleaners for dolls, handcuffs, necklaces, rings, basket handles. A child can spend hours arranging small pieces of felt—cut into circles, squares, triangles, rectangles—upon a twelve-inch square piece of felt-covered cardboard.

Four-year-olds love to sew large buttons onto cloth or cardboard. If you draw a picture such as a tree, they can put buttons on for bulbs and make it a Christmas tree. Make a person's head, and they can put buttons on for the eyes and nose.

You will also want play dough or clay. Be sure to stock several cans of powdered poster paint and a variety of brush sizes (the smaller your child, the bigger the brush). Children can paint old newspapers, old wrapping paper, butcher paper, cloth. Newsprint in sheets or rolls can be obtained from your newspaper office. For the child who makes many pictures, a place to keep his work is important. A simple envelope-type portfolio can be made by folding three sheets of newsprint and stapling along the two sides, leaving the top open. Write your child's name on the front and then let him add a few touches of his own. Expose your children to different kinds of painting—sponge painting, stick painting, potato stamping, spatter painting, and of course, finger painting.

When my children were small, we lived in a house with a glassed-in porch. Each child was given one window on which he could paint any scene he desired that pertained to the season. The "masterpieces" were left upon the windows for several weeks prior to the holiday. Then all joined in on helping wash the windows. This special showcase gave opportunity for others to see and admire the child's work.

Children love to make things with paper, and you can guide them in their fun by providing a variety of paper. Colored construction paper is a favorite. If this is not available, your child can color or paint his own. They can use paper to make chains, lanterns, fans, hats, airplanes, snowflakes, spirals, and whatever else their fertile minds can imagine. Be sure to supply plenty of paper bags to be used in making masks or puppets. Of course, puppets can also be made out of socks, clothespins, or peanuts.

Cardboard boxes are essential—big ones and little ones—to crawl in, under, to push, to pull, to put things in. Other things to save for your original creations are: oatmeal boxes, toilet paper tubes, wax paper tubes, egg cartons, shirt cardboards, wallpaper, paper bags, mesh bags, cottage cheese cartons, berry boxes, shoe boxes, coffee cans, old hose, jewelry, hats, feathers, buttons, spools, corks, and a variety of old magazines and catalogs.

If you do not take a "scrap craft" magazine, check with your local library to see if they have them. These magazines are full of ideas for creating all sorts of items from the above materials. Several such craft magazines are geared specifically toward the needs and capabilities of young children. Often the instructions are simple enough for young children to follow with minimal adult help.

WAYS TO WALK

We developed a variety of adventure-observation walks, named by the children. Then, when we decided to go for a walk, we'd choose one that fit the day and our mood. Some days we'd take a "color walk." We would choose a color before leaving home, then see how many things we could find of that color. This helped to sharpen the children's color perception.

Two favorite walks were "God created" or "man-made." Sometimes we would look for both on the same walk. When we did this, we would choose sides to see which team could spot the most things that were created by God or by man (from materials God had already created).

The result of these observations came to light one fourth of July. While watching fireworks, a small boy remarked to my son, "My dad made those." To which Terry quickly replied, "Yes, but God created the stuff so he could."

Another looked-forward-to outing was the "vehicle walk." The children would ride tricycles and wagons; or take their pull and push toys. A word of caution: This walk is not for days when patience is fleeting.

On one of our walks one beautiful spring day, we stopped to watch two birds building their nest. Later, I was telling a friend about the birds when Keith spoke up, "Yep, we were work watching." Thus our "work watching" walks came into being. Perhaps the workers we observed would be ants scurrying to an ant hill, a squirrel gathering nuts, a spider weaving a web, or men working on streets or buildings. But whatever we watched, we always returned home with a greater admiration for God's creatures.

If a poll were to be taken among my children, I suppose that the favorite walk would be the "collection walk." For this, each explorer was given a small sack into which he placed any "collection" of his choice which he spotted along the way. These could be pretty stones, leaves, bugs, acorns, flowers, whatever. Many pleasant hours would be spent examining these treasures after we arrived home.

Like most mothers I imagine you have days when you feel your vocal cords have been strained to the breaking point. When this happened to me, I'd announce a "quiet walk." At first the smallest tots found this difficult, but they soon learned how to play the game and took part willingly. The rules stated everyone must be silent on the walk. But on arriving home, each child could take his turn telling what he saw. These reports always gave me new insights into my children's thoughts and interests.

The next time you have the urge "to get out of the house," try one of these walks or create ones to suit you. How far you go and how much time you take is not important. It's impossible to measure the ultimate value of your walks. But if you desire closer companionship between you and your children and new zest in your life, walks are wonderful! So is going new places.

NEW PLACES

Talk to your children about the trip before you go. This may sound elementary, but it is important, especially for children under six. They won't be as liable to feel uprooted and will enjoy their experience more if they know what to expect. Show pictures and explain the different kinds of architecture they might see. Perhaps most of the new homes they will see will have stairways, while this may not be so where you live. Perhaps you will encounter hills or mountains, which your child may not have seen—or even a lake or an ocean.

You can talk about differences in people with unfamiliar life styles. You might tell about Uncle Joe who goes about in a wheelchair. Discussions along with pictures in story books or magazines can help your child become so familiar with the proposed trip that his anxiety will become anticipation.

Don't wait until you can afford some lengthy trip to travel with your child. You can plan special excursions regularly, such as a visit to the firehouse, or to a farm if you live in the city. Maybe you can arrive in time to watch the farmer milking his cow. Children enjoy a short ride on a local train, a visit to a pet shop, the five-minute car wash, museums, even factories where they make things of interest to them, such as ice cream or cereal. They might even enjoy watching a new house "grow." You don't have to go far to discover unexplored territory. You will soon see that these direct experiences will serve as touchstones for your child's new knowledge, upon which you can later build.

Camping is a favorite adventure for many parents with
small children. If you happen not to be a camping
enthusiast, your child can still experience camping in his
backyard. Bedrolls atop plastic become sleeping bags.
A piece of canvas or an old blanket can become a tent.
Better yet, if weather permits, let the children sleep
under the stars. Usually young children like to have one of
their parents or an older friend sleep out with them
the first time. They might even initiate the experience by
sleeping in the tent for their afternoon nap. If at all
possible, have a campfire and allow your child to enjoy the
fun of roasting hot dogs or making his own toast on a
stick over the fire.

MAIL MAGIC

"Mailman, mailman," sang Alice from her lookout by the
front door. Then she ran to me and watched as I opened
the box.

"How pretty, Mother! Where did you get it?" she
asked. "Why did you get it? It's not your birthday."

By then several small questioners were watching in
awe as I pulled a lovely valentine book out of the box.
"Grandmother sent it to Mother, just because she loves
Mother," I told them. Suddenly the day seemed brighter.

After looking at the book and enjoying the pictures,
Alice said, "I wish I could get happy mail with my name
on it."

Thus the idea of a family mailbox was born. For if
"happy mail" could change my day, why couldn't it do the
same for the children? We used an old mailbox. If
you don't have one, make your own with anything from a
shoe box to a lard can. You can decorate it and put it in a
special place, or hang it on the wall. In the summer
it's fun to have the mailbox outdoors.

You should establish the time of the day when the mail
is to be distributed. Do you have a youngster who
awakes from his nap crying, grumpy, or moody? I changed
such grumpiness by having our mailtime as soon as the
children awoke from their naps! (This sometimes helps

to coax them to go to sleep also.) And mailtime will never grow old if it comes but once a day.

Now for the fun—and fun it is! The junk ads you get in the mail—which you might hand to the kids anyway—can become personalized if you print the child's name on the envelope. You can also use cards, pretty pictures, old magazines, anything that will delight a child. Tiny gifts are extra special and should be used sparingly.

A three-year-old can make out his name on *his* mail, which makes him feel he's a very important person. My children often asked someone to read their letters over and over again. Some I sent were serious, some said only, "I love you," others would be used to teach.

For example, I had been asked to a politician's home for a meeting. A few days before the event, three-year-old David received a letter. In it was a picture of a lovely living room, complete with beautiful glass knickknacks. A small boy was sitting on the white sofa beside his mother. The letter read, "This boy is named David. He is a well-behaved boy. He goes to see some ladies with his mother. He does not run or touch things." Then a picture showed a dining table with cookies, milk, and coffee. The little boy was eating a cookie. The caption was, "The lady gave him a cookie. David said 'Thank you.' "

I'm happy to report that the little "catalog picture boy" was no better behaved than my own David. And that wonderful positive teaching was accomplished through our little mailbox game! As the children started school and began to read for themselves, the joy and helpfulness of these letters increased. Somehow letters don't nag the way mothers seem to.

Trish's bed usually had such a messy look. One day a letter came to her showing the picture of a neatly-made bed with only one stuffed animal lying on it. Underneath the picture was written, "I believe your bed could look as pretty as this one, if your animals and dolls would take turns lying on your pillow."

The next day there was a letter addressed to me in the mailbox. "Dear Mother, your rite. Go see."

Trish's letter started the two-way communications between myself and each of the children, as soon as they gained printing ability. Sometimes I received a question, a joke, an idea they might have, or just an answer to one of my notes. Most important, I had found another way to reach the hearts and minds of my children with fun, instructions, meditations, and love.

FIVE
HOW TO UTILIZE
SELF-FULFILLING PROPHECY

By the time a child is six years old, his lifelong
self-concept is congealed. This is based on how he
perceives attitudes directed toward him by the significant
persons in his life, primarily his mother. The correlation
between his first six years of life and his personality
and achievements as an adult is indeed great. Some
psychologists state that personality traits are fixed by the
age of two.

The first determinant is our genetic inheritance. This
provides everyone with his basic potentials, primarily
physical. Next is our environment, both physical and
social. Each plays an important role in the forming of our
personality. Last is the self-concept. I personally believe
this is *the* all-important determinant in any individual's
development.

It is in the home where your child becomes the kind of
person he perceives others think him to be: a success
or failure, worthy or unworthy. Your child has no other
standards for measuring his adequacy; therefore, the
family environment establishes the child's level of self-
esteem. As his mother, it is your responsibility to help
him develop his self-concept in a positive way.

Some random studies done by psychologists indicate
that the results of children's IQ tests could be affected by

the expectations of those administering the tests. The entire range of expectations and self-fulfilling prophecies was examined in the mid-1960s beginning with a controversial study of teachers' expectations of students. The children in eighteen classrooms were given a test disguised to supposedly predict "intellectual blooming."

After the test 20 percent of the children were selected at random and their names given to the teachers with the assurances that these children could be expected to show remarkable gains during the coming year. The only differences between the 20 percent and the other 80 percent of the children were solely in the teachers' minds.

Eight months later all the children were retested. It was found that those children identified as most likely to "bloom" did show a greater increase in overall IQ gain over the others. It was assumed that because the teachers *expected* some students to do better, they did, in fact, fulfill those expectations.

Psychologists have concluded that the concept is more than fantasy and that one person's expectations can influence the behavior of another. The phenomenon has come to be called "self-fulfilling prophecy," and nowhere is it stronger than in the mother-child relationship.

KNOW WHO GOD SAYS YOU ARE

Never depreciate yourself or your child, nor allow him to. Proverbs 6:2 says, "Thou art snared with the words of thy mouth," while Proverbs 18:21 declares, "Death and life are in the power of the tongue." In order to keep from being snared and speaking death to your child's self-esteem, learn never to say less about yourself or your child than what God says.

God says that he made you and your child, that you are wonderfully complex creations, and his workmanship is marvelous (Psa. 139). God says that you are created for *his glory* (Isa. 43:7). Jesus calls us his friends (John 15:14). God calls us joint-heirs with Jesus Christ (Eph. 2:6). "Faith cometh by hearing, and hearing by the

word of God" (Rom. 10:17). Faith in yourself also comes
by hearing what God says about you. And if you hear
regularly who God's Word says you are, you will soon
begin to see yourself as God sees you. God sees us as his
own handiwork, recreated in Christ Jesus, that we may
do those good works which he planned beforehand for us,
that we should live the good life which he has made ready
for us to live (Eph. 2:10, AB).

As your child begins to grasp how much God loves him,
how wonderfully he is made, and how important he is to
God, then his self-acceptance will grow. This is vital to
his desire to become a "son of God," and will help
him develop in a positive manner.

Another important facet of this foundation is teaching
your child to meditate on God's love. Help him memorize
and become familiar with verses which say or imply that
God loves him. Then just before bedtime every night,
review with him the way God loves him by quoting some
of the Scripture verses he has learned. For example,
as you tuck him in you could say, "Remember that
God said, 'I have loved you with an everlasting love' "
(Jer. 31:3).

"What is everlasting?" he asks.

"Never coming to an end."

"Does that mean God loves me that way . . . even when
I don't share my toys?"

"Yes, even then God's love for you just goes on always
and always. So when you're all snuggled down in your
bed, think about how nice it is that God has provided it for
you."

Practice exercises like this diligently with your child
so you can establish this as a pattern. (See Deut. 6:6, 7.)
As you begin to teach your child with the many words
of God's love, he will learn to let thankfulness be his last
thought before dropping off to sleep. And thus he will
sleep in a more restful manner.

Several times a week, write down the name of a person
(picture or drawing for the nonreader) who has verbally
expressed love for your child or who has done something
that implies he or she loves him. Write or picture

specific expressions of love that the person has shown. Put these on your child's bulletin board, thanking God with your child for that person and his love. This exercise will be a very important, continual reminder to your child that he is loved.

Much of the feedback a child receives in his early years is focused on the physical: "My, how big he is!" or "Isn't she beautiful!" The more a parent focuses on a narrow set of characteristics, such as intelligence or beauty, the shakier a child's self-esteem becomes. For not all beautiful people stay that way, and there is always someone who is bigger. It is important for you to provide a more broadly based foundation for self-esteem in your child.

ACKNOWLEDGE ACCOMPLISHMENTS

To help broaden that foundation for my children, and thus utilize self-fulfilling prophecy to help them develop a positive self-concept, I developed a visual aid. I called it, simply, the "Accomplishment Book." You can use a spiral notebook, or staple several blank sheets of paper together, using construction paper for the cover.

On the pages of this book, I'd clip and paste pictures from magazines that illustrated things a child could do. Then we would make a game of "reading" the Accomplishment Book, page by page. I started a book for each child when he was very young, as soon as he became interested in sitting up and looking at pictures.

I learned a fascinating fact: Even very young children recognize and mimic the activities they see in "the book." As each child was able to "patty-cake," wave "bye-bye," "kiss grandpa," etc., a picture was added for each new performance. The book became thicker and thicker with the passing of months as we added these "accomplishment" pictures.

A child feels proud of himself when he can turn to the page in his book that illustrates the activities he can perform. I learned it was good to continue the book through the elementary years as the child learned to read and do his multiplication tables. The book was an excellent visual tool to help him develop pride in his achievements.

For me, though, there was another even greater benefit: It helped me, the child's mother, keep closely involved with all he was learning to do. There was also a bonus benefit for the child: He learned to anticipate doing new and different things.

One mother with whom I shared the concept of the Accomplishment Book told how fearful her young son was of anything new or unfamiliar. He wanted to wear the same shirt to play every day, and he insisted on exactly the same kind of sandwich for lunch. Each day he had a familiar pattern to follow and was fearful of any deviation.

After struggling for some time with her son's problem (punishment and begging seemed to only aggravate the situation), this mother stumbled upon the marvelous tool of praise. She began praising her son for even the slightest indication of venturesomeness, no matter how timid or slight. The thing that mattered was not the result but *that he had dared to try.* She ceased being critical and praised him for every little thing, which in his case was very big indeed. She also made him a "Different Ways" book. It was patterned after the "Accomplishment Book" except that it showed the same boy doing things many different ways. As time progressed, the little steps of change began to be bigger and longer until they were the steps of a secure child reaching out to a way untried.

AFFIRMING PRAISE

In the second chapter I also mentioned some uses of praise, but at this point I will deal with the subject in more depth because the use of praise cannot be over-emphasized. Actually, the giving of praise to your children is one of the special privileges of being a mother. In Proverbs Solomon acknowledged this when he said, "A word spoken in due season, how good it is!" and, "A word fitly spoken is like apples of gold in pictures of silver."

Praise is like sunshine to the human spirit. People cannot flower and grow without it. Behavioral scientists such as Dr. B. F. Skinner have done countless experiments to prove what wise mothers have known for centuries. That is, any human being (or animal) tends to repeat an act which has been immediately followed by a pleasant result. Praise shapes behavior and aids learning. And the behavior-shaping effect is greatest if the praise is given immediately; any delay tends to lessen its power.

One day I heard my neighbor criticizing her children for arguing. "Can you never play peacefully together?" she screamed. Tiny Lorie looked up thoughtfully. "Of course we can," she said, "but you never notice us when we do."

Most of us need more bolstering than we get. To help me on those days when I need praise the most, I made myself a "Praise Box." This was a very pretty gift box in which I saved every note of appreciation anyone sent me. Now whenever I need encouragement, I open it up and read the contents. I have found that this always works magic on sagging spirits.

This practice worked so effectively for me that I decided to make a "Praise Box" for each of my children. I sent them praise notes through the "house mail" (see chapter four), and asked their grandmothers to post them occasional praise notes. I also made notes for their praise boxes from verbal praises given to them, picturing both the child's deed and the other person's response. When the children reached school age they began accumulating special notes from teachers. And whenever a special boost of encouragement was needed, we would hang a praise note on their bulletin board.

Another affirming idea is to take a picture of each child, then have each of his siblings write or draw a positive statement about that person. The statements can then be attached to the picture and hung on the child's bulletin board. Occasionally we did this with several children in the neighborhood. What a rewarding experience to give every child several positive statements about himself attached to his picture! This not only reinforces his own feelings of self-worth but also encourages the habit of affirming others.

A word of caution regarding the art of praising: It is possible to go so far in praising your child for good behavior that it will cease to be an encouragement. For instance, if your praise becomes manipulative flattery, the child will detect dishonesty in you and react dishonestly. If you say the child is one thing when he is not, he will behave in such a manner to prove you wrong. Children are far wiser than we sometimes credit them with being.

Here are some praise examples: Unhelpful praise— "Thank you for opening the door, you're really a big boy." *Child feels deflated* because he thinks about his brother who is much bigger than he. Helpful praise— "Thank you for opening the door, it is a very heavy one." *Child feels proud of a specific accomplishment* and therefore thinks that he is strong. Unhelpful praise—"I just looked at your toy shelf, and I think you are a very neat girl." *Child feels uneasy and unworthy* because she left her clothes drawer very messy. Helpful praise—"I just looked at your toy shelf, and I like the way you organized it. I think I will organize my knickknacks that way." *Child feels proud of a specific accomplishment* which translates into her subconscious that she is neat.

So let's get into the habit of helpful praising, and by looking for things to praise, cultivate a loving attitude and an observant eye—qualities which enhance all of our relationships.

BUILDING SELF-ESTEEM

A great obstacle to healthy self-esteem is doubt of one's own ability. If you constantly do for your children or keep them from doing what they could do for themselves —by protecting, spoiling, scolding, or punishing them— your children will be deprived of the experience of developing and using their own strengths.

The mother of Baron von Richthofen, Germany's well-known World War I ace, once said, "An easily terrified mother is a great obstacle to the physical development of her children. When Manfred was a little boy, I believe many of my friends considered me a rather careless mother because I did not forbid him and his brother from engaging in some of the feats they liked. I was then, and am still, convinced children can only become agile if they are allowed such freedom as will enable them to judge what they can safely demand of their bodies."

When one of my own daughters was five, she asked for the job of dusting the china in the china cabinet. Since she was so very young, my immediate reaction was, "No way!" But as I considered her request, it seemed that my values were in the wrong place. I was more concerned with a crystal glass that could be easily replaced than I was about a young child's self-esteem that would be injured if she were told, "You aren't capable."

My doctor told me of the method he used to help build his child's self-esteem and to show his appreciation for the boy's interests: He gave him a charge account at a hardware store! The reason, he told me, was because the boy was interested in building all kinds of things with his hands. To encourage his son, this wise father told him he could buy anything he needed for his projects. Of course his son gleefully took advantage of the offer. As a result, by the time he was a teenager the boy had become a very knowledgeable handyman.

You may not be able to provide such an unlimited account for your child. Even so, I believe most mothers could determine their child's needs or talents and apply this idea in a way that would encourage him.

One mother I shared this idea with had a young son who was not as interested in reading as she wanted him to be, so she opened a limited charge account at a bookstore. She told him that every month he would have "X number of dollars" credited to his account, and he could pick out as many books as he desired up to that amount. Her son's reading began to improve immediately, and his interest in a variety of subjects expanded.

I believe the more a child is encouraged to participate (even vicariously) in life styles and roles different from those of his own family, the more interested in life he is likely to be, and the more interesting his own life will become.

Remember that predestined growth in any area, whether physical, intellectual, or spiritual, limits and ultimately cripples. A familiar illustration of this is to be seen in the way certain young Oriental girls had their feet bound. The purpose was to limit their growth so they would develop petite, beautiful feet. The result was all too often crippling instead of beautifying.

If you refuse to take time to expose your child to the multitudinous options of life and don't encourage him to make the most of the attributes and opportunities God has given him, then you are just as surely "binding" that child's life as one who bound a child's feet. And the result will also be crippling or stultifying.

So begin early to express appreciation for what your child is and encourage him in all that he is capable of becoming. What he is when he is born is less important than what he does with himself afterward. The living conditions in which he finds himself are less important than what he does with himself within that situation.

Self-esteem is actually the result of a comparison between the way we are and the way we ought or want to be; thus, the more we are like our ideals, the greater is our self-esteem. The successes you enable your child to attain become the nutrients on which his growing self-concept feeds.

That effective character-building Bible teacher, Henrietta Mears, used to tell her leader trainees that every time she met a person, she would visualize a sign hanging on his or her chest stating, "My name is _____, please help me feel important." This is a positive exercise for every mother to remember.

CHARACTER TRAITS

Another exercise you can adopt for your child's betterment is to learn to identify positive character traits which are being misused. For example, if your child seems to be overly organized and impatient—he may possess traits which, properly guided, can produce an efficient person. If he seems to be somewhat indifferent to his own needs, nonchalant, almost a "dormat"—these traits can be cultivated into patience with others. If he seems wasteful or a spendthrift—these traits can be channeled into generosity, and, thus sharpened and focused, he may well develop into one of God's special givers.

Just remember that any negative trait your child might exhibit is usually corollary to a misused positive quality. And if you realize this, you can so highlight the positive quality that the negative character traits will soon dissipate themselves. But you must believe and act upon this truth, for it to become so.

Goethe, the German author, said, "If you treat a man as he is, he will stay as he is. But if you treat him as if he were what he ought to be, and could be, he will become that bigger and better man." And if this is true of a man, how much more so of a child.

Our beliefs become the compass that gives direction to our lives. Most of our beliefs are attitudes we have observed and absorbed until they have become an integral part of our automatic guidance system. From infancy, our parents have told us who we are and have provided us with the criteria by which to determine the course of our lives. By the time we reach kindergarten, we are beginning to internalize their value system. It is therefore inevitable that what we believe we're going to be (which we've learned primarily from our mother), we will become.

This means that the child who goes through childhood convinced that he is a failure is guaranteed to fail. And the chubby girl who believes she will always be fat, continues to be fat. The quiet boy who is certain his talkative brother is smarter, usually manages to prove it with his school reports. Therefore it is essential that a child be perceived by his mother as a potential rather than a problem, as possessing strengths instead of weaknesses, as bright and reactive rather than dull and unresponsive. Because it is then and only then that your child will thrive and attain to his full capabilities.

SIX
YOUR CHILD IS GIFTED

The more Scripture I read, the more I am impressed
by its solid psychological concepts. And high on the list
are those having to do with self-image. In the last chapter
we suggested that one of the most crippling emotional
illnesses one can have is a low or negative self-concept. To
be emotionally whole, a person must be self-accepting.
And your child cannot become self-accepting unless you
help him.

It is within the social setting of the family that a child
forms his self-concept and learns to love, because he
feels loved; or to hate, because he feels he is unloved. If a
child grows up without deep assurances of love, he will
program his mind to entertain such thoughts as, "no-one-
loves-me-so-I-must-not-be-worthy-of-being-loved-so-how-
could-God-love-me-I-bet-he-doesn't-really."

One assurance of love that you can offer your child is
special help in developing the gift(s) God has given
him. And if you teach him the importance and necessity of
these gifts, then your child will be able to project his
own self-acceptance in a way that helps others as well.

After one Sunday morning service, I was standing
in the back of the auditorium waiting for my son, the
preacher. I had been moved by the earnestness of his
delivery. Suddenly an attractive woman approached me.
"You must be very happy about your son," she said

rather wistfully. "You know, you should be thankful that
God blessed you with gifted children. None of my
four sons has any special gifts." With a choked sob, she
turned and went out the door.

She was gone before I could share with her what God
had impressed upon me a few days after my oldest
child was born. I was reading in 1 Peter 4:10 that day and
the words seemed to have a new significance as I read
them. "As each one has received a special gift," the
Word said, "employ it in serving one another, as good
stewards of the manifold grace of God" (NASB).

I began to search God's Word to find the meaning of
"special gift." My answer came in Ephesians 4:7, *The Living
Bible:* "However, Christ has given each of us special
abilities—whatever he wants us to have out of his rich storehouse of gifts." Then in 1 Corinthians 12, I rediscovered
Paul's list of these gifts which he compares to our physical
anatomy.

THE GIFT OF HELPING

One of these special gifts God was talking about is one
that is often overlooked: the gift of helping. I saw this
gift in action one Sunday morning as I was helping care for
a group of three- and four-year-olds. Two were coloring,
two were quarreling over a toy truck and three were
engrossed in playing with puzzles. Four-year-old Jody was
among them.

Suddenly, Jody put her puzzle down and watched the
two who were quarreling. Then she quietly walked
across the room and picked up a tunnel. She sat it down
between the two scowling children and showed them
what fun it was for them to sit on either side of the tunnel
and roll the truck through to each other.

By this time dark-haired Allen was sobbing. Eloise,
one of the colorers, had dumped his puzzle upside down to
retaliate because he had inadvertently sat on one of
her crayons. Jody quickly noticed this crisis too. She
brought Allen a tissue, sat down beside him, and patiently
began helping him with his puzzle.

I suddenly realized I was seeing a living illustration of the Apostle Paul's words in Romans 12:7 (TLB). "If your gift is that of serving others, serve them well," and again in 1 Corinthians 12:28 (TLB), where he mentions, "Those who can *help* others." This gift, I have learned, includes being of assistance or giving aid in any way that encourages, strengthens, or brings hope.

Now, lest we become confused with semantics, let me clarify something important: I was helping in the nursery because it was my turn. Little Jody was "helping" in the nursery *because she has the gift of helping.* There is a vast difference and it is vital that parents recognize the difference. If Jody's gift is ignored, in time it will be used only out of duty or for selfish reasons. Jody needs to be taught that God has given her a special gift, one described in the Bible. When this fact is carefully presented and understood, then Jody, even as a small child, will be able to comprehend the scriptural analogy of the physical interdependence of the body's various organs. And she will be able to accept without jealousy the different gifts of her friends.

THE GIFT OF SHOWING MERCY

Romans 12:8 describes another gifted person as one who shows mercy with cheerfulness (TLB).

I am going to draw a fine line here between the gift of helping and that of showing mercy by adding these words to the definition of the former: "Being of assistance or giving aid in any way that encourages, strengthens, or brings hope to those different from ourselves, such as the sick, elderly, maladjusted, crippled, or those in public disgrace."

I believe Paul was referring to this expanded definition when he wrote to Timothy, "May the Lord bless Onesiphorus and all his family, because he visited me and encouraged me often. His visits revived me like a breath of fresh air, and he was never ashamed of my being in jail" (2 Tim. 1:16, TLB).

Many of us are fearful or ashamed to visit jails,

embarrassed to visit the maladjusted, too busy for the sick and elderly. I don't mean to excuse us for any of these reasons; my purpose is only to help parents recognize the gift of mercy.

One of my daughters seems to have an affinity for all grandmothers and grandfathers. As soon as she could ride her trike, she would pedal off to chat and rock with some elderly neighbor. In the beginning, I assumed she enjoyed their attention, but by the time she was old enough to help bake cookies, I noticed a definite difference between her and her siblings. Trish always took her cookies to share with one of her "grand" friends. The other children took their cookies and shared or bargained with friends of their own age.

Trish's special gift increased as she used it, and one of her first jobs was working in a nursing home.

THE GIFT OF LEADERSHIP

As a trustee of our school board, I was once asked to spend a part of a day on the congested playground to observe some problems. I noticed a group of boys shouting angrily at a petite girl. The louder they shouted at her, the more defiantly she tossed her long blonde hair. Moving closer so I could hear the heated discussion, I realized the problem. The girl wanted to join their war game and the boys were refusing to let her. They were at an impasse when a slender, fifth-grade boy appeared on the scene.

"Quiet! You're wasting our time," he said. "You guys be the defenders. We'll give you two minutes to get ready. Lisa, you can be my first lieutenant. Now scram!"

There was muttering, but they scrammed.

"You have just witnessed one of our most difficult problems in action," one of the teachers said to me. "What Lee does or says is law. Some of the kids love him, many hate him, but they all obey him. I don't understand it."

I was unable to erase that scene from my mind because I realized I had seen on that playground a potential

Hitler or Moses. The direction in which Lee goes will depend largely upon how he is taught to view and channel this special gift he's been given.

Again the Bible speaks rather specifically on this subject. "If God has given you administrative ability and put you in charge of the work of others," it says in Romans 12:8, "take the responsibility seriously" (TLB).

Leadership traits aren't always as dramatically exhibited as in Lee's case. But if you begin to observe your children—even your toddlers—in group situations and notice which child is most consistently copied or listened to, you will usually notice the emergence of leadership traits.

THE GIFT OF CRAFTSMANSHIP

If you read Exodus 31:3 (NASB) where God says, "I have filled him with the Spirit of God in wisdom, in understanding, in knowledge, and in all kinds of crafts-manship. . . " and continue read through verse 11, you will begin to recognize the significance God places on gifted workmanship.

Somewhere between our race to live in space and our eagerness to achieve nuclear power supremacy, we seem to have forgotten the importance God places on dedicated craftsmanship. I wonder if we haven't emotionally and spiritually crippled many children because of it.

Joe is a skilled mason, a real craftsman. Many times he has added beauty to a place of worship with a stone planter or a brick wall. However, during the years when his personality was developing, he was never taught the value of his special gift, the ability to use his hands. Now as a mature adult he is unable to believe that the dedication of his gift is as important to the kingdom of God as that of his friend's songleading ability.

The gift of craftsmanship encompasses a wide variety of physical skills. Sometimes we're prone to separate gifts into secular and spiritual realms, categorizing the spiritual as having more value to the Lord's work. It is imperative that our children be taught that their personal

value to the Lord's work is not determined by the kind
of gift which has been given them, but rather by their
willingness to use that gift for the Lord.

When your child so skillfully took apart your sweeper
piece by piece and then reassembled it, was your reaction
so negative that you neglected to notice his mechanical
skill? Or did you then find something else to interest
and challenge him to work on? That same skill—if early
dedicated to God—could someday be used to put
together or repair a printing press for a missionary.

Do you have a child who never tires of being in the
kitchen? All of us have been blessed at some time by a
person with the gift of cooking. Do we sometimes forget
that Jesus met the people's physical as well as spiritual
hunger?

THE GIFT OF EVANGELISM

The Scripture verse, "Some have special ability in
winning people to Christ, helping them to trust him as
their Savior" (Eph. 4:11, TLB), clearly defines the gift of
evangelism. Once, for a period of three years, I held a
weekly Child Evangelism class in my home. For two of
those three years one neighbor boy never missed a
meeting. But the thing that impressed me most about
Darrel was that he never came without bringing someone
who had never attended before. From the day that
Darrel accepted Jesus as his Lord and Savior, he seemed
to possess a consuming eagerness to share the Good
News with everyone.

Many times we as parents are embarrassed by our
children's zeal. But we must be careful—while striving
to teach them "tolerant tactfulness"—to not squelch
in them what may well be the gift of evangelism.

THE GIFT OF GIVING

We often hear sermons on returning to the Lord a portion
of all he has given us, or of the blessings of giving
cheerfully to God's work. But the gift of giving is usually

found in combination with the ability to make and
distribute money for the cause of God. The Bible says,
"If God has given you money, be generous in helping
others with it" (Rom. 12:8, TLB).

We all know people who have the "Midas touch." It
seems everything they attempt turns to profit. I have
such a friend, who is the head of a large corporation. He
gives generously to missions around the world. Those
of us who are close to him, though, are aware of his
heartache and frustration. He has prayed for years that he
might be allowed to be an evangelist. He was not taught
as a child that all gifts are needful—just as all parts of the
body are needed. Therefore he has never been able to
accept the fact that God's special gift of giving is just as
important and necessary as that of evangelism.

Some children manifest the gift of giving very early.
David is the youngest of my five children. One summer his
older brothers and sisters had a vegetable stand in
front of our house. They wouldn't let David participate
because he had not yet started school and was therefore
deemed "too young" for business. The day wore slowly
away and the older children hadn't made a single sale. So
when they became hot and discouraged, they told David
he could watch the stand while they went swimming.
David promptly filled his little red wagon with vegetables
and pulled it down the dirt road to three of the neighbors'
houses. Can you imagine the shock of the older children
when they returned from swimming to find David sitting
beside his now-empty wagon, elatedly sorting out his
pile of coins?

In the first grade, David spent hours dipping toothpicks
into cinnamon, so he could sell them to other kids
at school. In second grade he made and sold stationery
even though he has no particular artistic skills. Another
time, he went around the neighborhood soliciting car
wash jobs. When he had obtained a number of regular
jobs, he hired two boys to work for him, and he
supervised. David is still young, but his moneymaking
adventures continue. A tremendous responsibility
rests on his mother to see that he is taught that this is a

special gift God has given him. And what a vital part
David will have in God's service if he allows God to
develop and use his gift.

These are only a few of the special abilities that God
gives "out of his rich storehouse of gifts." However,
they will help you to begin to search out and identify your
child's special gift. When you notice your child developing
certain characteristics which fit the scriptural definition
of a special gift, prayerfully seek ways to help him
develop it for God's glory.

Two parents, in particular, who succeeded in helping
their children with their special gifts, really challenged
me.

One was the mother of my daughter's earliest childhood
playmate, a boy named Jeff. Jeff was always helping
injured playmates or stray or wounded animals. I recall a
featherless bird the children were ridiculing until Jeff
took it home. He loved and cared for it until it was healed,
then he helped it learn to fly again.

Not once did I ever see Jeff's mother display any dislike
for the battered, defenseless creatures he brought
home. Instead, she always showed interest and support.
The family moved away from our community, and we lost
touch for a while. The next time I saw Jeff, he was a
teenager. He was at the county fair. Jeff was talking
animatedly with a friend he was pushing in a wheelchair,
a boy with no legs. I thanked God for a mother who
encouraged her son to develop his gift of mercy.

While I was in Chicago not long ago, an enthusiastic
cab driver witnessed to me so joyfully that I felt
compelled to ask him how he ended up being "just a cab
driver."

He grinned. "Well, the whole thing began when I was a
little boy, about twenty-five years ago. I loved playing
with toy cars. My dad noticed I loved my little taxis
better than the other cars, so he helped me paint all my
cars to look like taxis.

"Then my dad would pretend to be different people
riding in my taxi. He taught me how to share Jesus with
all of them. As I grew older, my love of driving and

my desire to be a cab driver merged. And it was those memories of playing the taxi game with my dad that made me realize God had given me a skill I loved. All he expected from me was that I use my gift for his glory."

My emotions were a mixture of shame and awe. Shame that I still retained some of my early-learned dual standards, and awe of a father who had taught his young son not only to value his mechanical and driving skills, but to use those skills in ways that would glorify God.

Even very young children can grasp the importance of each part of the human body. This truth is especially well stated in *The Living Bible,* which reads, "God has put the body together in such a way that extra honor and care are given to those parts that might otherwise seem less important" (1 Cor. 12:24).

If your child feels that his special gift is not as useful as someone else's, then share this analogy with him: Ears are funny little things sticking on the side of your head. We might think they aren't as important as hands, because hands can move in all sorts of ways and do many kinds of things. They can catch a ball, hold crayons, play the piano, build towers. But even though hands can do many exciting things, only ears can do special things . . . like listen to a kitty purr, or hear a best friend's whispered secret.

You see, God tells us in the Bible that he will give special honor to the parts of the body which people might think are less useful. In that same way, God will give special honor to those personal gifts some people think are not as important as others.

If someone you loved gave you a special gift, wouldn't you love that person even more? The same principle applies when a child learns early that he is unique to God, and that God has given him a very special gift. When he is made aware of this, his love for God will increase.

In 2 Timothy, Paul admonishes us to "guard [protect] well the splendid, God-given ability you received." *The Jerusalem Bible* says it this way: "You have been trusted to look after something precious, guard it with the help of the Holy Spirit."

SEVEN
TRANSFORMING THROUGH THOUGHT CONTROL

Every mind develops thought patterns over the years.
Whether these thought patterns are negative or positive
depends upon how you have programmed your mind. As a
mother you have the awesome responsibility of teaching
your child how to program positive thought patterns,
for this will essentially affect everything he is or does
in life.

Second Corinthians 10:5 tells us to "take captive every
thought to make it obedient to Christ." Philippians 4:8
(NASB) tells us how to do that: "Whatever is true,
whatever is honorable, whatever is right, whatever is
pure, whatever is lovely, whatever is of good repute, if
there is any excellence and if anything worthy of praise,
let your mind dwell on these things."

Every mother needs to be aware that her child's
specific attitudes and emotions are determined by his
perceptions, which are learned primarily from his mother.
In a study of preschool children, psychologist Lafore
reported a consistent relationship between maternal
behaviors and children's attitudes and emotions. He
found that a mother neutralizes or heightens the trauma
in a child's life; and, contrary to what many people
believe, fears are not inborn or instinctive. Fears
are acquired through a condition or association. And the
mother's own adjustment creates an aura of either

insecurity or security which envelops the child. So the effect of trauma or fear on your child will depend upon his perception of the situation as learned from his environment. Environments (or mothers) that magnify situations into traumas usually cause a child to develop a pattern of negative attitudes.

Webster defines attitude as "the state of mind behavior regarding some matter." And the Word of God tells us to "be transformed (changed) by the [entire] renewal of your mind—by its new ideals and its new attitude . . ." (Rom. 12:2, AB). Therefore, if attitudes are a state of mind and God tells us to renew our minds, that means we do indeed control our attitudes.

FEAR ATTITUDES

There is no reason for a child who is taught to love and trust the Lord to be fearful. We are told that peace is given to us through Christ . . . "freedom from fears" (1 Pet. 1:2, AB). We early teach our children Psalm 23:4, which says, "I will fear no evil, for you are with me." King David is saying, "*I* will not fear evil." He declares that he is making a decision, a choice in his mind. This is precisely what Philippians 4:8 means when the writer tells us to fix our minds on non-fearing thoughts.

You see, attitudes are more important than facts. And it is *what we fix our minds on* that creates the attitude which causes the fear. It's only when we allow our mind to become fixed on frightening things happening around us, that we become fearful. Because, "God did not give us a spirit of . . . fear—but . . . of power and of love and of calm and well-balanced mind and discipline and self-control" (2 Tim. 1:7, AB). Sometimes it is easier to be fearful than to have faith in what God has said.

God has said that we are not to have anxiety or distraction about anything, for he has given us his peace. How? Through knowledge of him (2 Pet. 1:2, AB). Jesus says to us, "Peace I leave with you. . . . Do not let your heart be troubled, neither let it be afraid—stop allowing yourselves to be agitated and disturbed; and do not permit yourselves to be fearful and intimidated and cowardly and unsettled" (John 14:27, AB). In this verse "heart" ("Do not let your *heart* be troubled") is the word *kardia* in Greek, and can be correctly translated, "the heart, the thoughts or feelings, mind."

So, if the Scripture is true, to be fearful or not is an act of volition. I cannot control the thoughts that come into my mind, but I can control what I think about, what I fix my mind on. Therefore, to inculcate this principle in my children, I must learn and know the promises of God and teach them to my children. You and your children can repeat them over and over again, forcing your minds and thoughts to practice what you are learning.

The mind is such an effective therapeutic instrument that numerous physicians are now using imaginative visualization to aid medicine in emotional healing. One such example is that of a little girl who was afraid of many things and people and felt secure only when she was holding her father's hand. Dr. Jampolski helped her to expand her imagination about her father holding her hand so that whenever she had these fears, she could *visualize* her father holding her hand. The girl learned that the visualized security of holding her father's hand enabled her to look at each new situation without being so frightened or threatened.

Most of us have heard or read about the power of positive thinking. Positive thinking is a spiritual idea, because thinking positively means to shift your thoughts from the things that are *against* you, and focus them on the vast power that is *for* you. Always remember that he who lives in you is greater, mightier, than he who is in the world (1 John 4:4).

ATTITUDES TOWARD HEALTH

Whether or not your child becomes a hypochondriac is largely dependent upon your own attitude toward illness. And I believe there is far too much unnecessary illness. My personal philosophy comes directly from

Scripture, which tells me that if I attend to God's words and submit to his sayings, then his words are life to me, healing and health to all my flesh (Prov. 4:20-22).

It is extremely important how a mother behaves when her child tells her he does not feel well. Do you cuddle the child more when he doesn't feel well? Do you unnecessarily wait on him? Do you entertain him? Do you spend more time loving him? If so, then you are, in fact, reinforcing in your child's mind the idea that it is better to be sick than well. When your child does not feel well, he should, of course, receive adequate care, but not to the point of indulgence. Instead, extra loving, time, and attention should be given to the *well* child. That will reinforce the idea that it is better to be well than to be sick.

ATTITUDES TOWARD FOOD

One day when we were having stew again, I heard the grumbling grow louder as I started dishing it up. I turned to the children and said, "Lots of boys and girls would be thrilled with your bowl of stew."

Alice smiled sweetly and responded, "Why don't you send them mine!"

Times like those make a mother wonder how she can teach her children to be thankful for food. Most people, and this includes children, tend to favor certain foods and dislike others. And often the disliked foods provide necessary nutrients. As I pondered this problem, I arrived at the "no-thank-you helping" plan. And it worked. In practice this means that everybody will be served and will eat a small spoonful of even the food he thinks he dislikes. By doing this, my children learned to like things they thought they never would. Note: This no-thank-you helping is not to be confused with requiring a child to clean up his plate which has been laden with more food than his body needs.

Another means I used to encourage children to eat everything on the menu was the "favorite supper" night.

For that meal one member of the family was allowed
to choose the menu. The children loved this idea and
would eat willingly of everyone else's favorites, knowing
their own turn would be coming soon. This plan has
a special bonus. Allowing even the youngest child to
help plan the menu makes him more aware of the
many different kinds of food which he will want to taste.

Keith never liked tomatoes until I let him plant some
one year. He watered them every day and tended them
very carefully. When he picked the first tomato, I asked,
"How would you like it fixed?" He enjoyed it and
has been eating tomatoes ever since. I realize that
gardening won't always cure food dislikes, but it will give
your children a greater appreciation for food and God.
Gardening will also help them to see the necessity of
various kinds of weather, so that one day when you've
planned a picnic and it begins to rain, you may hear a
small voice say, "Thank you , God, for watering my
carrots."

Here's a principle that should be inviolate: Never use
food for a reward. By so doing, we become responsible
for allowing our children to become slaves of food.
How does this happen? By giving a child food when he
falls and hurts himself—to make him feel better. By
giving food as a pacifier when he is not allowed to do
something he wants to do. Or by giving food for comfort
when he is sad for some reason. When we reward our
children in these ways we are teaching them that food is a
panacea for all hurts, wrongs, or illnesses. This can
soon cause a child to become psychologically addicted to
food. This is the very thing King David asked God to
do to his enemies when he prayed, "Let their table
become a snare and a trap."

Your child will never become an overweight adult if he
is taught to think correctly about food. The Apostle
Paul could have had food in mind when he said,
"Everything is lawful, but I will not become a slave of
anything or be brought under its power" (1 Cor. 6:12,
paraphrased).

ENTHUSIASTIC ATTITUDES

The word "enthusiasm" comes from the Greek, *en theos,* which means, *in God.* So, of all people, who should possess a greater degree of enthusiasm than those of us who claim to be "in God"?

Learn to become excited about your daily work. An enthused mother who gets excited about her daily work can make any mundane job an elevated position. Frequently I hear mothers say, "If only I had a *glamorous* job I could get excited. If you knew how difficult it is for me to stay at home with the children, you wouldn't tell me to learn to get excited about my work."

I always remind such mothers that work, wherever you find it, includes the same ingredients: detailed monotony, preparation, striving, and weariness. Life everywhere is so *daily.* But that is the attitude that we all have to overcome, no matter what our work is.

Most of us find it easy to get excited about something that somebody else is doing. But when I have that job to do, and must learn and grow and plan and persevere— then it's work. There is nothing that can make you more excited about your work than a sense of that work's importance. Not the importance of the work I wish I could do, or the work I'm going to do when the kids are grown, *but the work I am doing now.* And I, with millions of other mothers around the world, can testify to the glaring truth that if you botch the job of raising your children, nothing else you achieve in life will really matter very much. Being a mother is important: to your child, to your community, to your country, to his world.

There is no other way to learn to be an enthusiastic mother than to become totally involved and committed to the task you are engaged in. Behave as though every aspect of your life is a job worth doing and your attitude will soon fall into line with your behavior.

It's true that some people are naturally outgoing, gregarious, and enthusiastic; but for those to whom enthusiasm does not come naturally, it can be cultivated. To do this means to consciously put your eyes, your voice, your spirit—in other words, yourself—into your appreciation of your family. You will be surprised at how quickly this becomes second nature.

You begin by learning often to say something positive to every member of the family. When Judy spills her milk, hand her the sponge and express appreciation for the way she helps you clean up.

Have you noticed that for many people, as much as 95 percent of their conversation is negative? I'm talking about downright pessimism. And I am fully convinced that there is nothing that will improve the atmosphere and productivity of your home as much as *you:* the enthusiastic mother who provides positive words and a positive outlook for her family (always remembering the message of Proverbs 18:21, "Death and life are in the power of the tongue").

Actually, if you habitually cultivate the habit of projecting positive attitudes to your family and others, it won't always be necessary to speak. Your very presence will carry a positive atmosphere wherever you go. In 2 Corinthians 7, Paul talks about such a positive atmosphere that was created by Titus' presence. He said, "Then God who cheers those who are discouraged refreshed us by the arrival of Titus—not only was his presence a joy, but also the news that he brought of the wonderful time that he had with you."

Ask yourself the question, "Does my presence refresh my family?"

Learn to see something positive in daily situations. Have you ever noticed how quickly our minds leap to the negative conclusions about things we see and hear? When Sally comes into the house and says, "Guess what Billy did?" do you respond, "Is he in the street again? Or did he throw rocks at the neighbor?"

Then we should be chagrined at our negative thoughts when Sally replies, "No, he shared his cookie with the neighbor!"

The best thoughts in life don't come easy. They come free, but not easy, for we must consistently cultivate them. Remember: If you really want to create a positive attitude, you can. It *is* possible. Frequently, though, the problem is that we don't really want to make the effort.

But if you begin doing this at home, you will soon find yourself living in a more gracious and enthusiastic world. For your enthusiasm will be reflected back to you from your family.

BUILDING ATTITUDES

Attitudes toward people and situations make us what we really are. And attitudes are a matter of habit. How then can we make our attitudes conform to the kind of person we want to be? By deciding—in line with God's Word—the kind of person we want to be; then by training our mind to become that person. In 2 Corinthians 10:5 it says, "Take captive every thought to make it obedient to Christ." Colossians 3:2 (AB) says, "Set your minds and keep them set on what is above—the higher things." God is telling us to make his words a part of our thought life. If we decide to do that, our decision becomes a behavior commitment. And behavior commitment changes attitudes. This is an important commitment, for once you make it, you will find yourself involved in one of the greatest warfares of your life.

Concentrating on your thoughts in fighting this inner war becomes crucial. In any conflict, including this one, one must come to a thorough understanding of the strengths and weaknesses of the opposition. In this battle our unruly emotional attitudes are both violent and elusive. This is their strength.

So we must deal with the causes of these attitudes by cutting off their supply lines. And that source is our undesirable thought patterns.

The reason for this is that the mind and the flesh with its carnal thoughts and purposes is hostile to God, for it does not submit itself to God's law. So if you are living the life of the flesh, catering to the impulses of your carnal nature, you cannot please God or be acceptable to him.

The good news is that we are not obligated to live a life ruled by the standards of our carnal nature (sarkikos,

the Greek word translated "carnal" in the King James
Bible, literally means "body-ruled"). But we can, through
the power of the Holy Spirit, habitually put to death,
make extinct, the evil deeds and thoughts prompted by
our body and mind (Rom. 8:7, 8, 12, 13).

Do you want to cultivate the attitude of praise? Then
read the praise Psalms to your children over and over
and over again. Read them aloud until they sear
themselves into your spirits. Record a cassette with praise
songs, psalms, grateful statements. Give your child a
small cassette recorder to take to bed with him. Let him
fill his mind with these thoughts as he drops off to
sleep.

Praise your children and others. Verbally acknowledge
them for their excellent qualities or for jobs or deeds
well done. Be specific. Don't say, "Mary, you've been
a good girl today." But rather, "Mary, thank you for
helping me today by picking up your toys." Or, "Mary,
you were very thoughtful to share your tricycle with
Susie when she doesn't have one."

*Do you desire the attitude of consideration for yourself
and your child?* Then, "None of you should think
only of his own affairs, but each should learn to see things
from other people's point of view" (Phil. 2:4, Phillips).
A very young child can learn the truth of this verse.
For example, take a golf ball that is half white and half
another color, say red. Hold the ball, or let one of your
child's friends hold the ball, so that your child sees
only the white side. Then ask, "What color do you think
this golf ball is?"

He will, of course, respond, "White."

Then you ask the other child, "Judy, what color do you
think this golf ball is?"

She will say, "Red."

This gives the opportunity to talk about how one may
see or understand something differently than another. But
that does not mean that either of you is wrong. It
simply means you have different viewpoints. You develop
the attitude of consideration by learning and accepting
that.

It is possible to bring about any attitudinal change

in your life that you desire, by making a behavior commitment to set your mind (and keep it set) on God's words.

Oh, the joys of those who do not follow evil men's advice, who do not hang around with sinners, scoffing at the things of God. But they delight in doing everything God wants them to, and day and night are always meditating on his laws and thinking about ways to follow him more closely (Psa. 1:1, 2, TLB).

It's important to consider the things we allow to dwell in our minds. How often do you or your children "hang around" (with people, TV, or literature) to relax and rest, where the scoffers gather? Everything you read and hear affects your train of thinking. Joseph Fort Newton expresses this so very well:

Every person has a train of thought on which he rides when he is alone. The dignity and nobility of his life, as well as his happiness, depend upon the direction in which that train is going, the baggage it carries, and the scenery through which it travels.

For reinforcing biblical principles, for stimulating imagination and increasing language perception, a great deal of reading is essential. Since children naturally model your actions, they will become readers if they often see you reading. By the time a child is two he will accept a pictureless book to hold, if you are holding one— especially if you then read or quote Scripture to him. If you do this every day, you will soon hear your child's voice importantly "reading" along with you.

By carefully choosing reading material, we can help our children keep their thoughts on whatever is true, whatever is noble, whatever is right, whatever is pure, whatever is lovely, whatever is admirable and whatever is excellent or praiseworthy.

A book of poems should be a must for every family. Children love all kinds of poetry, not just nursery rhymes.

And until taught differently, they won't consider poetry dull or difficult; children soon learn to love the rhythm, the cadence, and the beauty of words rightly put together.

I believe the reason my oldest children early learned to appreciate and enjoy the books of Psalms and Proverbs, was because of their love of poetry. How they delighted in finding a poem or proverb for every occasion. I recall going to the planetarium with Keith's second grade class, and upon seeing the stars lighting the ceiling of the room, Keith's first statement was, "The heavens declare the glory of God." His brother David, who was three, whispered in my ear, "Twinkle, twinkle little star, God made you, there you are!"

Whether David had been told those words or had made them up, I don't know, but neither boy had been frustrated by an inability to verbally express himself, because each's reading appetite had been whetted through wide selections of good reading material.

An aunt of mine once told me, "If you want help in rearing your children, use books as bees use flowers." Since bees work individually and as a unit, I decided that our reading would have to be done both alone and as a family. So luncheon always found my preschoolers and me with a book on our table. As they ate, I read them a story. It is amazing the obedience children will give to the suggestion of a storybook character, and the way they grasp a simple moral that may have eluded our adult "superior" learning.

As obscene literature proliferates, I believe the best way for us to fight it is by bringing good literature into our homes. Give children a love for good reading from the beginning of their story-listening years and you won't need to be concerned about the books they choose as young adults.

A short time ago, I read in a current magazine, "Whatever happened to the family dinner hour?" The article spoke of the diversions of modern life which have helped to destroy this fine tradition in many homes. Then the author asked, "How can we bring it back?"

Is this a problem at your house? Do your children jump

up as soon as they have finished eating? Do you look
at sullen faces when your children are told, "Stay in your
chairs until everyone is ready to leave the table?"
If the answer to these is yes, you might try this enjoyable
answer: For dinner this evening, along with the meat,
vegetables, salad, and potatoes, give your children
something more, a wider vision, a greater dream, an
upward look, a joyous approach to learning. Serve them a
chapter from a first-rate book.

Mothers sometimes ask me, "When do you find time to
read?" Well, in this age of time-saving gadgets, I have
found books the greatest time-saver of them all. If you
have a book handy, you will never waste those precious
minutes that slip away so quickly. Carry a book in
your purse or pocket. Teach your children to always have
a book with them, and they will never grow restless
during those unavoidable times of delay.

We carry a small box in our car in which we place our
"traveling" books. Once you've tried this yourself,
you won't go without it again. Reading while in motion
does not affect us, so we spend much profitable time this
way. On long trips, time passes quickly when someone
is reading aloud. We use these books to read during
periods of waiting: in the car or at the doctor's or dentist's
office.

Keep books in every room. If you are in the kitchen
with a few minutes to spare, chances are you won't
take time to look for a book that's in another room on a
bookshelf. But if there's one in the kitchen at your
fingertips, you will probably pick it up. How about the
bathroom, dining room, bedside table? Some of these
places may seem amusing, but if books are laid around the
house invitingly, you and your children will read
much more than if they are kept only in neat rows in the
bookcase.

Such a practice encourages reading more than one book
at a time. If you have never tried reading several books
before finishing one, you should. We talk with more than
one person in a day, so why shouldn't we read more
than one book during a day? Besides, your mood changes.
In the morning, some thought-provoking book may

appeal to you; while in the evening, you may relish something lighter. By reading in this way, you will find yourself finishing more books than when you make yourself read through one before starting another.

Schedule visits to the library on your child's calendar. Be sure to plan ample time for him to browse, enjoy the librarian's story hour, and choose his books. "Enjoying the library" is a learned activity, so make sure each child has his own library card and plenty of time to *enjoy.*

Books are invaluable sources of learning that can teach your children the high ideals and principles you wish to impart. Thus it is important to devise ways to get your child to read appropriate books. This is especially true if he seems not to be interested in them. I solved this problem by paying my children to read.

I chose books that would inspire or teach history, a moral, a vision. Or books that would motivate them. These books I would label with different "price tags" and place on the children's bookshelves. When a child completed a book I would require an oral report before payment was made.

One day when my youngest son was fifteen, his older brother came into his room and looked at the priced books. He pulled one off the shelf and asked, "David, how much are you getting for reading this book?"

"Five dollars."

"Five dollars! When I read this book I only got a quarter!"

David laughed. "Inflation has even hit the family bookshelves."

Proverbs 22:6 tells us that we should whet our children's appetites for the things of the Lord. Imagine this word picture of an ancient Hebrew midwife who was responsible for the baby's care and keeping: If the baby resisted nursing, the midwife would dip her finger in olive oil and gently stroke the roof of the baby's mouth. This would create a desire to nurse. The Hebrew word for "train up" refers to this gentle stroking action. This is how God desires every mother to train her child's mind: by whetting his appetite for the words of the Lord.

EIGHT
LEARNING TO
COMMUNICATE EFFECTIVELY

Basically we communicate in four ways: by what we do,
how we look, what we say, and how we say it. Human
communication includes how we dress (see chapter
three), how we sit, the gestures we use, even the amount
of space we need around us. We project a certain
"body language," which is a part of the discipline called
kinesics. Kinesics comes from the Greek word *kihema*—
motion. It describes the communication that comes
from every part of one's person.

Some scientists say kinesics is so important that the
emotional impact of any message is 55 percent facial,
38 percent vocal, and only 7 percent verbal. That means
your body sometimes talk louder than your mouth.
It also means that if your body is contradicting your words,
your child will find it difficult to understand or believe
your words.

If such a large percent of the emotional impact of
any message I give to my child is facial, that means my
smile is very important. And contrary to popular belief,
facial expression can be trained. Such training must
begin with pleasant thoughts that prompt pleasant
expression, which then must be deliberately practiced.
The more you practice both the pleasant thoughts and
their expression, the more spontaneous they become.

Here's an exercise you and your child can do together to develop your smiling muscles: Look into a mirror and smile the biggest, broadest smile you can muster. Hold that smile by tightening your facial muscles. Your fingers can feel the tightening of the muscles and the skin on your cheeks and under your jaw. Do this as often as you can. The more your smiling muscles are exercised, the more easily they will react to a spontaneous signal. Even as you help your child to teach his hand muscles how to hold a pencil and tie a shoe, you can also help him teach his face to express a happy look. There's a bonus to be gained by such practice: When a smile starts on the face, it usually spreads to the spirit.

Another important aspect of a facial message is eye contact. Good eye contact means that your eyes meet the eyes of your child in such a way as to express the same message that your words are conveying. The eyes help give the warmth of feeling to symbolic words. Maintaining good eye contact is a learned behavior.

To help my children feel comfortable with direct eye contact, we played a game we called "Gaze." The rules are simple: Two people sit opposite each other and gaze directly into each other's eyes for a predetermined length of time. Begin with just a few seconds with participants about a table-length apart. As the child improves, lengthen the time and shorten the distance. By playing with a timer, you can have two winners instead of only one—if both hold steady to the end.

VOCAL IMPACT

You've put a smile on your face; now put a smile in your voice! Remember a smile can be heard as well as seen. In our home we placed a mirror next to our telephone and I trained the children to smile into the mirror before picking up the phone. This practice caught on so well that when one of the children would call home to ask special permission for something, he would often say, before making his request, "I'd like to hear the smile in your voice, Mother."

Learn to keep monotony out of your voice. This is usually not a problem when one is angry. But do you make it a practice to express yourself with varieties of pitch and tone during normal conversation? One of the best ways I know to actually "hear" yourself, then actively work on improving the speaking quality of your voice, is to make tape recordings of yourself, then play them back.

One semester when I was teaching English to ninth graders, I had each of the students tape a reading. The most frequent comments were, "I didn't know I sounded like that," and, "I don't want to sound like that." Most of us have no idea how we sound to others. That's why I believe that the purchase and use of a tape recorder is a very worthwhile expenditure. In fact, it is difficult to improve oneself without one. And since our small children must listen to our voices constantly day after day, we should make an effort to offer them the most pleasing sounds we can.

A tape recorder can also become one of your most delightful teaching tools. Children love to record their voices. Such tapes not only become good keepsakes, they also make lovely gifts for grandparents. And a message of either praise or reproof from Mother via the tape recorder is more palatable than it would be in person.

VERBAL IMPACT

Be enthusiastic in your choice of words. Sprinkle your speech with descriptive words and emphasize them with the inflections of your voice. We can best help our child to use colorful speech by being graphic in our own phraseology. We should be sure that we have the precise idea we want to convey clear in our own mind before trying to communicate it. Develop the habit of using words that accurately portray a picture for your child. For example, "a brown and white collie" is more descriptive and accurate than to say merely "a dog."

Whenever we use a word that could have more than one meaning, we should explain both definitions. One day when Alice was quite young, she spent the afternoon with some of our Amish neighbors who were washing the "globes" of their lamps. When Alice came home she was troubled about her friend calling those glass things globes when "there wasn't one single country on them!" So we started a "Words-do-such-different-things" chart. Later we expanded the chart's usefulness to identify words with more than one meaning, unusual definitions, and strange-sounding (to the child) pronunciations.

Such expanding knowledge made it necessary for each child to have a dictionary suitable for his ability. Even preschoolers can contribute to the "Words-do-such-different-things" chart. When Trish was four she put the word "yak" on the chart because she said she thought it was a funny way to say, "talk-talk-talk," but her dictionary showed the word as "a big, big scary ox." Keith then put the word xylophone on the chart, because the picture beside the word looked just like an instrument we had in our house. We called ours a marimba, which certainly didn't start with an X. Both of these examples are simple applications of the benefits of helping children learn to enjoy the fun of words.

It's especially important to have a dictionary and thesaurus close at hand for your own use. And as soon as each child begins looking at books and learning to read them, he should have his own personal dictionary and thesaurus. At first he should use simplified versions, of course. But as soon as he "outgrows" them through reading more advanced books, his reference books should grow to meet this need.

A child should be taught how to use these books. After carefully showing him the mechanics of the books, you might begin with simple "dictionary" drills. These can be similar to the Bible drills you probably took part in when you were younger. Each participant would hold his Bible loosely between his knees. A reference would be given, then the leader said, "Draw swords. Charge!" Each person would then open his Bible and see how quickly he could locate the verse and read it.

This same procedure can be used very effectively with dictionaries. Since children of most ages enjoy competition, this is an exciting, yet painless way to learn how to use a dictionary, as well as a way to become familiar with meanings of new words.

Of course, dictionaries are sold everywhere: in drugstores, supermarkets, chain stores, and bookstores. Some are good, some not so good. Before you buy one, look up some familiar words in several different dictionaries. What do you think of the definitions? Are they clear and accurate? Which dictionary has the best illustrations and maps? Which has the clearest, most legible type? Naturally, you will want to choose the one best suited for your child.

Now that your child has his own dictionary, teach him how to use it. As he grows older, introduce him to his dictionary's distinctive features. Does his dictionary indicate word origins? Show him what they mean and how important they are. Does his dictionary have an appendix? What does it include?

Since correct pronunciation is such an important aspect of our verbal communication, teach him to use the pronunciation guide in his dictionary. It is much easier to take time to teach a child how to pronounce and use a word correctly to begin with, than to reteach him later. It is important never to laugh when a child mispronounces a word. But take the necessary time (in private) to instruct him in the best use of the word.

You can easily help your child develop the dictionary habit by demonstrating its use yourself. When your child asks a question such as, "How many pints are there in a gallon?" instead of immediately answering, "eight," say, "Let's look it up!" Your children will soon learn to enjoy looking up pronunciations to see if they can catch you mispronouncing a word.

An atlas is another must as a home reference book. Show your child how to read the maps; how to choose the route for a weekend trip—which way is shorter, which one is likely to be more monotonous, which one is a back road or a surfaced road. Often your car insurance company will make this type of atlas available to you.

Don't overlook almanacs and books of facts. Though such books are usually printed for adults, they can be enjoyed very much by young children. They are a universal source of information and provide stimulus to a child's imagination; they enable him to increase his knowledge and interest in his world and the world beyond his scope of experience. Almanacs give biographies of presidents, names of congressmen, descriptions of foreign countries, geographical data on the highest mountains, longest rivers, etc. Of course, if you are looking for a more complete book of facts on the highest, longest, fastest, etc., you will look for the *Guinness Book of World Records.* Most children are delighted with that book.

Many parents ask, "Should we buy a set of encyclopedias? If we buy it when our children are three and four, won't it be outdated by the time they are old enough to use it?" Not really. Some entries will be obsolete, of course, and the very latest inventions and newborn nations would not be included. But by far the vast majority of the material in encyclopedias does not change over a period of years.

Encyclopedias tend to whet the curiosity of a child; they encourage him to research information on subjects of interest to him. Encyclopedias can also help set straight misinformation your child may get from friends or TV. If a child has encyclopedias in his home, he will learn to view them as friends, rather than as a threatening mass of words that must be used for schoolwork.

All of these suggested aids are also vocabulary builders. And who among us doesn't at times experience a paucity of words with which to express himself? The Chinese have a saying: "He who strikes the first blow concedes that he has lost the argument." Often when a child (or an adult) is angry, he becomes physical when he cannot adequately express himself verbally. By helping your child increase his vocabulary, you will increase both his self-confidence and his self-control.

Last but not least among the verbal skills is good grammar. Many of us have enjoyed the play, *My Fair Lady*. The story tells of a linguist who teaches a lowly cockney flower girl how to speak correct English to enable her to become a lady. Though the story is amusing, it projects the serious underlying principle that one's language capabilities help define his world. And it is during a child's early years that we begin setting the parameters for the world in which he will most comfortably function.

CONVERSATION BASICS

Most children need help in learning the basics of conversation: What is it and how do I do it? An aid to teaching the basics of conversing well is a game I call "Catch Talk." To begin, seat your child on the floor, toss him a ball, and have him toss it back. Toss it back and forth a few times. Then toss the ball and tell the child to keep it in his lap. Toss another to keep in his lap, then a third and a fourth. Then put your hands in your lap and sit there. The child may become somewhat uncomfortable, thinking it's not much of a game. He may even say, "We're not playing now."

"That's right," you say, "we're not. In order to play catch ball, you have to catch the ball, then toss it back to me. It's the same with Catch Talk. When someone throws you a sentence or question, you have to catch it and throw one back. Let's try it.

"If I asked you if you had fun at Sandy's yesterday, what would you say?"

"Yes."

"Did you play with his trains?"

"Yes."

"Did you remember to thank Mrs. Rath for inviting you?"

"Yes."

Now stop and go back over the questions and answers by tossing a ball with each question and instructing your child to keep it in his lap. Then explain how he had

also caught the talk-balls by answering, yes, but had
not kept them moving by throwing a talk-ball back.
Suggest that you try the first question again.

"Did you have fun at Sandy's yesterday?"

"Yes."

"OK, you've caught the ball. Now what could you say to
throw a talk-ball back to me? How about telling me
one thing you played?"

"We played with his dog."

"What fun that must have been. Mrs. Rath told me that
Sandy's dog does tricks."

"Yes, he plays dead, sits up, and brings sticks back
when you throw them."

"That makes a fun game, just like the fun we're having
by throwing sentences to each other to catch and send
back."

Your child will immediately see the connection between
the two "games." The skill of conversing is like other
skills in that it requires practice to artfully participate.
So practice—it's fun.

EXPANDING TABLE CONVERSATIONS

The main purpose of table conversation is to provide
positive stimulation, so that the child will anticipate coming
to the table as a place to feed his mind and spirit as
well as his body. Emotionally disturbing talk should never
be allowed at the table.

In order to stimulate table conversation I often used
quizzes that I adapted from a weekly IQ quiz our
newspaper printed. Though most of these questions were
too difficult for preschoolers, I discovered that they
were not only easy to simplify but that they were also
interesting to a wide range of ages. Another table
conversation prop I used was made by cutting a picture
from the daily newspaper and discussing the story it
contained. Once a week the children would bring their
takehome Sunday school paper, their *Weekly Reader*
(when they went to school), or a story from a subscription
magazine to the table. I would allow them to read or

tell the story they selected, then answer questions from the rest of the family.

Asking questions that force children to react—by disrupting their standard thought patterns and accepted routines—is an excellent formula for exchanging knowledge and communicating emotions. One way to do this is with a "what" question. For example, ask what the child thought it would be like to be a farmer on the island of Haiti in a village of 300 people. What would it be like to be the farmer's son?

"So what" is next. What does the farmer's son do differently in his day's activities than I do in mine? What choices does he have? How are they different from mine? How would he view my home and my life? What kinds of things might he understand that I don't? What would it feel like to be that Haitian boy?

Next come the "now what" questions. Would Jesus Christ make a positive difference in the Haitian boy's life? If so, name the differences. Do I have a responsibility to help reach him with the good news? If so, exactly what is my responsibility? A caution: It is better not to use the "now what" questions unless you, as a mother, are prepared to help with very specific answers.

There's a communicative benefit to be derived by mothers who learn to ask insightful questions of their children: By their example and encouragement the children learn to reciprocate. This is good, both for accumulating knowledge and for enhancing communication. Never refuse to answer a question. And never knowingly answer a question incorrectly, either deliberately or in ignorance. To do so would result in the corrosion of your child's trust, and it is impossible to establish true communication without trust.

There are numerous books to help you with those difficult questions that all children think about and often ask. One is *Why Did God Let Grandpa Die?* by Phoebe Cranor (Dimension Books, Minneapolis, Minn.). This book quite adequately handles sixteen frequently asked questions, including the title question.

Other stimuli for expanding table conversation include

techniques for reading, discussed in chapter seven. Dinnertime can also offer an excellent forum for recitations. At this time anyone who had memorized anything of note could expound, being assured he would receive both the attention and applause of the whole family. Because children enjoy being the center of attention, these occasions are a great encouragement for them to practice memorizing.

Another way to encourage memorization is to use the finished product as a gift. The idea first occurred to me when Terry was eight years old. As my birthday drew near, he became concerned about what he could give me as a gift. I suggested that he memorize one of my favorite poems, "Somebody's Mother." Terry's first objection to this idea was, "But no one will know that I gave you anything." So to correct that wrong assumption, our dinner table performances were born.

Through the years as my children grew older and began to memorize more and more of the written words that had molded my own thinking, I noticed that we were developing a very close communion. As the children's thought processes were being enhanced by the assimilation of good literature, we were all beginning to perceive life from a mutual point of view.

It takes planned effort to make your dinner hour a meaningful communication event, but it's worth it. At our house, whenever the children left the table they were required to say, "May I please be excused?" Upon receiving an affirmative answer, they then said, "Thank you for the lunch (breakfast, food, etc.)." They were not required to add descriptive adjectives, such as *good* lunch, *yummy* food, unless they chose to. But one evening Trish, who was five at the time, said, "Thank you for the delicious dinner and the delicious talking." At that moment I knew the effort was worth it.

WHAT DID HE REALLY SAY?

When your child articulates an event or situation, you should be more concerned with his underlying feelings or

attitudes than with the actual "what" of the words he
expressed. For example if he were to say, "You gave
Johnny the biggest piece of pie," or, "You gave me the
little one." It does little good to remind him that Johnny
is two years older than he or that Johnny's piece was
not much larger than his own. The true issue involved is
more likely, "Mother, do you love me as much as you love
Johnny?" The truly listening mother might respond to
the questioner in two ways. First with words, "Were you
wondering about my love for you?" then with a reassuring
hug.

In order to really communicate when you converse with
your child, you must first listen to the words he says;
second, determine exactly what was behind his
verbalization; and third, continue the conversation in
such a way that you are able to prove to him that you
understand.

Mothers all too often ignore a child's feelings, fears, or
craving for sympathetic understanding which may be
hidden in his words. For instance, Ralph may not know
how to spell very well. So when he says, "I am terrible in
spelling," and you answer with, "Yes, you are a poor
speller," all you are doing is affirming his ignorance.

But if you really heard what he was saying, you might
answer something like, "I remember when I was your age,
I missed three out of five words in a spelling contest—
and one of them was 'which.' I spelled it 'witch.' But I can
spell that word today and many, many others. So I know
you will also be able to spell well someday." Ralph was
doubtless hoping to receive your encouragement and
assurance of faith in him when he made the statement in
the first place.

Every communication involves some kind of emphasis.
Unfortunately our school system frequently chooses
a negative one. For example, a child's paper usually
emphasizes the number of wrong answers rather than the
number of right answers. But if you will consistently
emphasize the positive with your preschooler, you can
materially lessen the effect of negative communication
which he will eventually receive from others. When

you play games with right or wrong answers—whether written or verbal—always announce your child's number of right answers instead of wrong ones.

Another method which can help develop effective communication with preschool children is use of a reversible doll. There are several of these on the market, but ours had "Little Red Riding Hood" at one end and "Grandma" at the other. When Grandma's nightcap was removed you would find the "Big Bad Wolf." Some mornings the children would take turns holding up the doll personality that best portrayed how they felt. If a child held up "Little Red Riding Hood" it meant he felt loved and happy. If he held up "Grandma" he was telling me that he was going to be a good worker today. Therefore, I would ask the child who had communicated his willingness to work to do the extra tasks that day. But if he held up the "Big Bad Wolf," the child was telling everyone he felt a bit grumpy—like the wolf—and therefore needed extra loving.

One of the most helpful things I discovered about this means of communication was the way the other children responded to the child who held up the wolf. They would each go out of their way to be especially nice and thoughtful to the one who felt grumpy, giving him an extra hug or sharing a favorite toy.

WHAT IS YOUR CONFESSION?

When you read the words confession and profession in your Bible, remember that they both come from the Greek word *homologia*. The literal translation of the word means "to say the same thing as another," or, when used in the New Testament, "to say the same thing God says." This means we are to confess or speak everything the Word of God says we are, what we have, and what we can do. Hebrews 10:23 reminds us to "hold fast the profession of our faith without wavering; for he is faithful that promised." By so doing we communicate power and strength to every situation.

Words are the most powerful things in the universe. People who say they *can* do something and those that say they can't are both right—because you are snared with the words of your mouth (Prov. 6:2). They become self-fulfilling prophecies. The kind of words you speak and teach your child to speak are important. Words are like little seeds that produce after their kind. Jesus said that by our words we shall be justified and by our words we shall be condemned (Matt. 12:37). Mothers, we must become word-conscious!

The spoken word of God is creative power. When God spoke, the world came into being. (See Gen. 1.) The universe is maintained by the word of God. (See Heb. 1:3.) The natural world is to be controlled by man speaking God's words. (See John 14:12-14.) All through the Bible, the spoken word of God came first, then the physical manifestations. " . . . God, calleth those things which be not as though they were" (Rom. 4:17).

You communicate your faith (or lack of it) to your child by the words your child hears you say. "Faith cometh by hearing and hearing by the word of God" (Rom. 10:17). Therefore the secret of a growing faith is in continually saying what God says—about everything.

For example: You are going to have a baby and your present income is not sufficient to support another person. You can either choose to talk about the seemingly hopeless situation and all its ramifications or you can say, *"God says* that if I seek him first then all these other things shall be given to me" (Matt. 6:33); and *"God says* that he will supply all my needs according to his riches" (Phil. 4:19); and *"God says* that he is my Shepherd, therefore I shall not want" (Psa. 23:1); and *"God says* that this book of the law 'shall not depart out of [my] mouth' but I shall meditate on it day and night . . . for then will my way be made prosperous and I will have good success" (Josh. 1:8). A confession of faith does not mean that you don't continue to do whatever you can to better the circumstances, nor does it deny the circumstances, but regardless of the circumstances continues to say what God says about every situation. You see, circumstances change but the Word of God does not change. And God is committed to prospering his Word. " . . . yea, I have spoken it, I will also bring it to pass" (Isa. 46:11).

God's words are true and filled with faith, and when we confess them (say them aloud), they cause our faith to grow. Your faith and the faith of your young child will never rise above the level of your confessions—the words you speak. And that makes it incumbent upon you not only to know the Word of God but to teach it to your child: "Precept upon precept; line upon line, here a little, and there a little" (Isa. 28:10). Chapter twelve deals with methods of teaching God's Word to your child.

In the book of Revelation (chapter 12), we are told that Satan accuses the believers before God both day and night. But verse 11 of that same chapter tells us that God has provided a twofold offensive weapon with which we can overcome Satan whenever he attacks: "By the blood of the Lamb, and by the word of their testimony." No wonder we are told in 2 Timothy 2:16 to "avoid all empty (vain, useless, idle) talk, for it will lead people into more and more ungodliness" (AB). As mothers we are responsible for the kind of talk our young child hears and participates in. And if we are using idle (that means noneffective or nonworking) words then we will lead our child into ungodliness.

Mothers have tremendous control over the kind of communication a child receives about himself and his world. Perceptions formed in the early years also affect the way subsequent information is interpreted. This means it is of vital importance that you, the mother, choose not only appropriate information for your child, but also appropriate words. Jesus said, "For out of the abundance of the heart the mouth speaketh" (Matt. 12:34). And the words you fill your child's mind and spirit with will be the abundance out of which he communicates with his world.

REDEMPTIVE LISTENING

It was one of those dreary, nappy days. I had been lying down for about fifteen minutes when I heard loud voices in the next room.

"I just want to tell you something."

"I don't have time to hear it. I'm the mother, so you
listen to me."

Alice and her doll were having a conversation and I was
suddenly painfully aware of the truth that whatever
a child is learning, he will incorporate into his play life.
And I wondered, is this what she is learning from me?
It wasn't just the tone of voice—cross though it was—nor
the forcing of the younger to listen. It was the fact that
while I was trying to teach my children to listen to me,
I might be forgetting the importance of listening to them.

Earlier that same day one of the children had asked,
"Are you sure God hears me?" At the time I judged
that he was concerned about God's capabilities. But I
wondered now if he was perhaps wondering how God
would have time to listen when his mother so seldom did.
Wide awake now, I realized I had been making a pretense
of listening, while my mind was busy with the day's
schedule. I remembered how often I would quickly say,
"Why don't you go play?"

I knew then that it was not enough simply to *act* like a
listener, I needed to *be* a listener. A good listener
listens to understand, really understand, what the other
person is saying. Too frequently mothers and children do
not communicate: they merely take turns talking. I
didn't want that to happen to me, so I began to write down
methods for improving myself as a listener. First I
wrote things not to do: do not disagree with the first things
said, do not start preaching and advising, do not take
over the conversation, or interrupt, or change the subject
before the speaker feels himself understood.

Some of the do's I wrote for myself were: *Be interested.*
This will help you to really understand your child; then
you will truly project an attitude of *wanting* to listen.
This attitude will free your child from restraints and
enable him to talk more easily.

Listen with your whole body, not just your ears. Look
directly at him. Watch his expressions. Don't just
hear words. Sit or stand attentively. Even lean forward
at times. Look as if you are enjoying listening. Raise
eyebrows, nod head, smile, laugh when appropriate. And
above all, maintain good eye contact.

Let your child tell his tale. Then ask appropriate
questions. "Where did this happen?" "What color was the
bug?" "Is this what you mean?" Repeat what he said,
putting it into your own words. Add meaningful
comments, such as, "I didn't know that. Thank you for
telling me or teaching me something today." Remember:
The asking of *good* questions represents listening on the
highest plane.

In chapter five I talked about ways to help a child
develop a positive self-concept. One not mentioned there
is the parent's listening. A child's self-concept is
threatened when his mother does not listen and greatly
improves as she *learns* to listen. A topic that is much
debated is whether we as mothers have a greater effect
on our children by the way we listen or by the way we
instruct. I believe we need a good balance of both.

Plan your day to include listening times. When my four
oldest children had gone to school, David began to
interrupt me frequently throughout the morning. So we
set aside time each midmorning for our "milk-chat." This
was to be his very special part of the day during which
he received my undivided attention. After we had
established this ritual, David seldom interrupted me while
I was busy. If he found a picture he wanted to share
or a pretty stone to show, he would lay it on the table for
our "milk-chat."

Planned talk-times are helpful to your child, and
usually lead to continued confidences in years to come.
Another rewarding aspect is the new way in which your
child begins to listen to you. And if you begin listening
to your preschool child's ideas, after he becomes a
teenager he will not close his mind to you.

I realize, of course, that there are some things that
just can't wait until later to be shared. If at all possible,
whenever the children arrived home from anywhere, I
would make myself free to listen. And I've learned that
there are few tasks that can't be set aside for a few minutes
of listening.

God says, "Be still, and know that I am God" (Psa.
46:10). How can our children be still and know, if they

haven't learned to listen? How can they learn to listen, if they haven't been listened to?

High prices are paid to a psychiatrist for his "listening ear," but real listening is always costly. Real listening costs unhurried time. It requires patience, love, and understanding. It asks that you learn to see into the soul of your child.

NINE
TODAY'S DREAMS BECOME TOMORROW'S REALITIES

Creative imagination is a part of the mind that generates desires, thoughts, hopes, and dreams. Everything that has ever been achieved started first as an unseen spark in a creative imagination. "In the beginning God created . . . ." God spoke into existence his imaginings. He created man in his own image and gave to mankind the gift of imagination so that we can also form, hold, and achieve images. Then when Jesus came, he liberated man's imagination by telling him, "I assure you that the man who believes in Me will do the same things that I have done. Yes, and he will do even greater things than these" (John 14:12, Phillips).

As a mother, you may stunt the growth of your child's imagination unless you dare to believe that what Jesus said is true. Uncontrolled imaginations are more likely to act negatively than positively. All of our problems in living are rooted in our imaginations, which we have power to control. "Casting down imaginations, and every high thing that exalteth itself against the knowledge of God, and bringing into captivity every thought to the obedience of Christ" (2 Cor. 10:5).

Letting one's imagination run wild can be one of the most destructive forces in life; but we don't have to let our imaginations run wild. Instead, we can, "Roll [our] works [transactions, activities] upon the Lord—commit and trust them wholly to Him; [He will cause your thoughts to become agreeable to His will, and] so shall your plans be established and succeed" (Prov. 16:3, AB). Often people succeed because they expect to succeed and fail because they expect to fail.

When Keith was in his year of freshman college studies, he wrote a new song entitled, "Expect the Best." This is known as "creative expectancy."

VICARIOUS IMAGINATION

This part of our imagination enables us to put ourselves in the place of others. The use of this ability is the key to the development of persuasive human relations skills.

A good way to expand your child's vicarious imagination is to have a "role" chest or cupboard. Fill it with every possible type of clothing—hats, purses, shoes, belts, old curtains, etc. These items will shout out suggestions to your child's imagination and they will help make already-written stories come alive. What better way for children to learn that the people of Bible stories are real than by acting out the lives of those characters in a play. Older children can use the actual Bible words for their characters when possible. Much Scripture is memorized this way.

My Sunday school class of first graders often got restless when we reviewed the last week's lesson. It seemed as though they never remembered the things I had tried to impress upon them. One Sunday as we finished the story of Queen Esther, I asked, "Who wants to be in a play next week?" Every hand went up. I assigned a part to each child, giving him the biblical reference from which his mother could read about the person to him. I promised to bring appropriate clothes for them to wear for the "play." When they departed, each child was eagerly anticipating next week's lesson. The following Sunday the amount of enthusiasm generated by the children was immense. Not only did they know their parts, but some of them could actually recite word for word what his character had said. The appointed Haman even knew what a gallows was. I doubt that any of those children ever forgot the people in the book of Esther!

My five children loved to "play church" from the time they were old enough to walk. For this high event, they arranged seats and benches with every stuffed animal and doll in the house. The "church's" tiny pianist (appropriately dressed, complete with wobbly, high-heeled shoes), pounded away at her instrument. The song leader in a long white shirt and a tie led the singing. All the while the preacher, in a pair of shoes six sizes too large, stood nearby tapping on the makeshift pulpit, eagerly awaiting his turn to "preach."

Sometimes after reading a story or telling about a family in history, the children would choose which one of the characters they were going to be. After choosing roles, we would playact the story as it was read or told. A variation they loved was to playact the story as "What would you do or say if you had been there?"

Sometimes we would have musical programs. For these I would put on a record: something classical, a march, perhaps a spiritual, or even a waltz. As we listened to the record, I'd ask the children what feelings and ideas the music gave them. After we had talked about it, I suggested, "Let's see if you can be some of the things you can hear in the music." This occasioned a trip to the "role" chest to locate and don the appropriate items they needed to express what the music said to them.

Have you ever seen a little airplane with scarves streaking behind, taxiing onto the runway, rising into the air and soaring through skies—all to the rhythm of a Viennese waltz?

Yet "flying into space" was only one of the many ways my children's minds were released to explore through the medium of creative music.

Our music room has been transformed—through their imaginations—into a huge rain forest filled with wild, wild animals. It has been a vast sea in which tiny boats bobbed and great ocean liners sailed. And it has been a simple tree on which busy caterpillars crawled, soon to cocoon themselves and emerge as lovely butterflies.

To be a participative partner in the innovative creations of her children is one of the most enriching experiences a mother can possibly have.

INTUITION: ARCHITECT OF THE BRAIN

Standing in line at the supermarket one day, I heard a mother say crossly to her little boy, "Make up another story like that one and you'll spend the rest of the day in your room."

As I listened, I wished I could tell her about the experiments of Robert McKim, Professor of Design Engineering at Stanford University. He created what he calls an "imaginarium" for the purpose of tapping the vast unknown riches of the mind's eye because he was concerned about finding ways to expand his students' thinking about design problems. McKim's experiments led him to design his own version of a geodesic dome which serves as a special environment where people can get away from noise and other distractions. "The person who learns to use his or her imagination flexibly," McKim explained, "sees creatively."

We must remember that the brain is divided into two distinct parts, each having different functions in areas of influence. The left side of the brain is basically concerned with the logical and the verbal: it thinks. The right side of the brain is related to the intuitive and creative: it knows.

For example, imagine a long Amtrak train moving down a railroad track as seen by two people, Randy and Nancy. Randy is standing on the ground about three feet from the track and is looking directly ahead at the train as it passes. Out of the corner of his eye, he can glimpse that part of the train which has already passed as well as that part which will pass momentarily. Most of what he sees is what is passing right in front of him from moment to moment—the engine, then the first car, then the second car, and on and on until finally the caboose has come

and gone. This is the way the left or logical side of the
brain functions.

Nancy is watching the same train at the same time. She
is up high in an air balloon. From her vantage point
above the train, she perceives it entirely differently from
Randy. Instead of seeing the Amtrak one car at a time,
she sees it all at once. This all-at-once (intuitive)
point of view is the way the right side of the brain
functions.

It is the right side of the brain that we tend to neglect.
All too often we admonish our children to stop daydreaming. How many times have you said to your
children, "Find something to do—don't just sit there
staring into space."

Pearl Buck said in *My Several Worlds,* "How sorry I
feel nowadays for the overcrowded lives of my own
children, whose every hour is filled with school, sport and
social events of various kinds. They have no chance
to know the delight of long days empty except for what
one puts into them when there is nothing to do but what
one wants to do. Then the imagination grows, like
the tree of life, enchanting the air."

In order to help your child utilize all of his potential,
one side of his brain should not be developed while
he neglects the other. Learn to develop both in equal
relationship.

FANTASY IS FOR REAL

Mothers need to be aware that daydreaming can be a very
constructive mental exercise. The creative response
happens in a state of relaxed attention. It is in this state
that we have access to our images. The images that
emerge spontaneously from the inner self are fleeting and
easily forgotten, as we know from our experience with
dreams. So we should talk with our children about their
imaginings as frequently as possible. Learn to capture
thoughts from the unconscious, so you can then look at
them and work with them. Then teach your child to do
the same. After talking with your child, jot down his ideas

and fantasies. This will say to him that his ideas
and dreams are important. This translates in his mind
that he is important.

Dr. Jerome Singer of Yale University has done
extensive research on imagination and the lack of it in
children. He says, "Children's ability to make believe
helps them more sharply to distinguish between what
is real and what is fantasy. The more children develop
their imagination, the richer their lives can be expected
to be."

The preschool years are the best time for the child to
develop the habit of talking to God in continuous
conversation. As adults we often make our times of talking
with God a separate thing, rather than a part of every
conversation. But a young child who has learned to talk
with God as a best friend will develop an awareness of
God's presence which will remain throughout his adult
life.

The rejection of imagination, in favor of what we call
the real world, is so deeply ingrained in our culture
that our children's creative spirits have been all but
squashed in the name of education. Pablo Casals put his
finger on the problem when he said, "And what do we
teach our children in school? We teach them two-and-two
make four, and that Paris is the capital of France.
We should say to each of them, 'Do you know what
you are? You are a marvel; you are unique. In the
millions of years that have passed, there has never been
a little child like you.' "

Pretending and make-believe are special qualities of
human experience because they provide us with a
sense of God-given, mysterious, and powerful capacities.

We must plan a right time and place in order to obtain
the best results when playing the "Imagination Game."
Two conditions will help. The first is the absence
of distraction. But an even more important condition is
the desire to play. Completely voluntary participation
may not always be necessary for reading stories or
playing other games, but it is indispensible for imagination
games. If any player is reluctant, put off playing until
later.

CAN YOU IMAGINE THAT?

Libraries have books with fantasy games that delight children and broadly exercise the imagination. For example, this one from Richard DeMille's book, *Put Your Mother on the Ceiling:* "Fill your head full of water/have the water spray out of your ears/have it spray out of your nose/have it spray out of your eyes/have it spray out of your mouth/have the water go back into your ears/ have it go back into your nose/have it go back into your eyes/have it go back into your mouth/have it spray out of all those places again/have it go in again/what do you want to do now?" (As you read or quote the lines to your children, pause at each slash to allow time for the fantasy to become fully formed in each child's mind).

FEELINGS

Young children enjoy imagining sensations such as the feeling of feathers tickling their face, a weight pulling the arm down, a gas balloon pulling the arm up. Teaching your child to recall feelings is a first step toward recalling pictures, which will help him become a better reader. Try "feeling pictures" such as a running horse, an itch, the sound of rain on a roof, kicking a can, the taste of toothpaste.

A different type of feeling game comes from displaying inanimate objects such as a donut, flag, apple, leaf. Let your child choose to be one of them and then tell how he would feel if he were that object.

Colors always solicit feelings in people. Use a color chart or make one of your own. Let your child tell you which is his favorite color (this will change from time to time). You will gain new insights into your child as he tells you how he feels about that color.

STORIES

Freely use imaginative stories. One way to do that is to have the child choose the title and the mother tell the story, or have the mother choose the title and the child tell the story. Make sure your titles are imaginative ("The

Cow That Won't Moo," or "The Day It Rained Up"). Your child will have no trouble being quite creative if you affirm him in his ideas.

Other times, when you are reading a book to your child, close the book halfway through and ask your child to finish the story. After he has told his version, open the book and read the author's version. Then you can talk about the differences between your child's ideas and the author's ideas. This is not a time for value judgments, but simply a time for differentiating between ideas.

Other stimuli for imaginative storytelling are sound-effect records, which you can purchase at most record shops. Children can invent delightful tales from listening to these records.

SOCIAL STUDIES

By the time your child is five years old he will enjoy being a TV newscaster. Help him gather objects or pictures that will remind him of the day's or week's happenings. Then, right after supper, let him treat the whole family to a newscast. "That's the way it was at the Smith house today!"

Read articles in newspapers and magazines to your child on any suitable subject that he can comprehend or be interested in. A child who exercises his imagination early gains insight and comprehension skills. After reading about a situation that is printed in a newspaper, ask your child what he thinks should be done about it— what he would suggest. Then write an appropriate letter to the person involved, giving your child's opinion and letting your child sign his name. Almost every time my children did this, they received a positive letter in return. This does two things for your child. Once again he is assured that his ideas and opinions are important; second, he early becomes an active participant in his world.

SCIENCE AND MATHEMATICS

Even science and mathematics are dependent upon imagination. Delving into these areas can be surprising and exciting. At the very lowest level of inventiveness, three things can happen: awareness, identification, and association. The *awareness* of many developments that quietly but constantly occur. The *identification* that lays the base of comfortable expectations. The *association* that helps your child know why.

Let your child dismantle a clock or a mechanical toy. After a thorough examination period, ask him to tell you what he has observed and noticed.

Learn about static electricity by rubbing balloons with different materials.

Give him a quart jar with all sizes of measuring cups and spoons. Then allow him the fun of learning how many ways a quart can be made up.

The first time one of my sons was asked in school what makes up a quart, he responded by saying, "Two cups, eight tablespoons, and three 1/3 cups!"

Suggest to your child that he try out various ways that people communicate with one another, such as Braille, the musical notation system, Morse Code, symbols used by pilots on planes, Indian smoke signals, the manual alphabets for the hard-of-hearing. A young child will very quickly learn most of these and invent some more on his own.

One of my neighbors frequently had her children draw pictures of a machine that could do a job they didn't personally like to do. Her boys have become so adept at this type of creation, that you and I will probably someday use a machine they have invented.

Another favorite at our house was the product-improvement task. To do this you set out one of the children's toys. Everyone spends time looking at it, touching it, and trying to think of the cleverest and most unusual way this toy could be changed so that it would be more fun to play with.

PICTURING IT IN YOUR MIND'S EYE

Alex Morrison, famous golf instructor and author of *Better Golf Without Practice,* enables golfers to eliminate ten or twelve strokes from their scores through mental practice. Morrison demonstrates the correct swing and gives a few pointers in the area of golf. Then he asks the student to spend at least five minutes each day relaxed in an easy chair, eyes closed, picturing himself on the golf course playing the game perfectly.

"You must," says Morrison, "have a clear mental picture of the correct thing before you can do it successfully. That can be acquired through instruction, by watching championship golf or studying action pictures of golfers you admire."

One reason mental practice so often brings a prompt inprovement is that for the first time, instead of struggling to remember many isolated, confusing ideas, you have a complete pattern for performing. This is why books showing your preschool child how to do tasks he is just learning, such as tying shoes, buttoning shirts, correctly holding crayons, are so important. Teach your child to study the pictures, the illustrations, then close his eyes and picture it in his mind's eye. The more proficient he becomes at this, the more quickly difficult tasks become easy.

The part of your mind that plays the greatest role in achievement is that part of your mind that imagines. We spend years developing the part of our mind that stores knowledge, reasons, memorizes and learns, but almost no time in developing the immense potential of our imagination. Yet the untapped power of our imagination is almost unlimited.

Our imagination is a rich source of ideas and mental pictures that can be developed. A person's imagination reflects an ability to visualize something that has been neither seen nor experienced before. With your help this can become a reality in your child's life. Then his imagination can become his most cherished faculty. This will enable him to realize that God "is able to [carry out His purpose and] do superabundantly, far over and above all that we [dare] ask or think—infinitely beyond our highest prayers, desires, thoughts, hopes or dreams" (Eph. 3:20, AB). So help develop your children's ability to dream—that God may channel his dreams through them.

TEN
GOAL-SETTING:
A STATEMENT OF FAITH

Many mothers become frustrated when goal-setting is
mentioned because they assume it has to do with
management of time. And that, of course, is impossible!
You cannot "manage time." But you can learn to manage
yourself. You see, it's really incorrect to say, "I don't
have time to do that." You *do* have the time. You just do
not choose to spend it in that activity.

It is self-defeating to continually feed frustrations and
anxiety about time into your subconscious. Time is
what your life is made of. It's sweet and precious. The
Bible says that we should "redeem the time . . ." (Eph.
5:16), and we can do that through the management
of self by the use of goal-setting. All great achievers have
been great planners. They have developed the ability
to organize their activities, sort out the trivial from the
important, and invest their time in productive, meaningful
effort. For when there is no orderly planning for the
use of time—and the disposal of time is left to chance or
expediency—chaos will soon reign.

The common denominator among mothers who have
"enough time" is *thoughtful planning.* Perhaps the idea of
goal-setting through self-management is so simple
that it escapes many mothers, which causes them to get
uptight about "time." Actually, using time effectively
is basically dependent upon just one thing—the daily

identification and prioritizing of the things you have to do. You must decide which of your goals are the most important, then establish daily priorities to enable you to attain them.

Goals take the emphasis off the problems of the present and enable one to focus on future possibilities. Goals help me establish where I have been, where I am going, and what to do next in order to arrive. Proverbs says, "We should make plans—counting on God to direct us" (Prov. 16:9, TLB). Therefore goals are my statement of faith.

GOALS ARE MEASURABLE

In order for us to begin thinking on the same wavelength, I want to define what I mean when I use the word goal. To some people the words purpose and goal are interchangeable. However, in my usage, there's a very basic difference between purpose and goal: measurement.

A purpose is something for which we ultimately aim. It is not necessarily measurable in itself, but is a direction toward which we wish our life to move. Some examples could be: to give glory to God; to have a God-honoring home; to live by Christian standards; to be a good mother. But if all our life is centered only in purposes, we may never be able to tell if we have accomplished anything, because we have no way of measuring a purpose.

Purposes can set the direction for our life, but we need to define the steps that will enable us to accomplish those purposes. On the other hand, goals must be stated so as to be measurable in time and quantity, and—when needed—the steps for achieving them.

Let's try a little quiz to see if we are straight on this. Which of the following are purposes and which are goals?

1. Be a more gracious person.
2. Read at least one story to Jill every day of this week.
3. Buy Randy a new brown jacket.
4. Do some sewing this month.
5. Plan this month's weekly menus on Thursday evenings.

Answers: Number two and five are goals. They both include the necessary time limits and quantities needed to evaluate them. Number one has neither. Number three lists a quantity but no time limit. Number four has a time limit but no quantity, for we don't know if "Do some sewing" means making a new dress or doing some mending.

All of us have goals of some kind for our lives. Some of these goals are major and may extend for years into the future (such as putting a child through college or writing a book). Other goals may be immediate and minor (getting the baby's bottles boiled before his next feeding). Usually numerous minor goals are required to reach a major goal. A person who continually fails in achieving the minor goals is likely to experience difficulty in achieving his major (long-range) goals.

This would then mean that such a person would also be unable to achieve what he considers his purpose(s) in life. For instance, one of the examples of a purpose in this chapter was to be a good mother. Obviously such a purpose would mean something different to each mother. But if this is *your* purpose, you must decide what it means to you and then list the necessary goals to enable you to stay on course. One such goal might be to give an hour a day of undivided time to your child, another to set aside a regular amount of time for devotions geared to your child's level of comprehension, etc.

CHART YOUR GOALS

One of the most helpful exercises that I have discovered is to think about what I would like to be, to be doing, or to have accomplished fifteen years from now. Such an exercise is a good one to explore by fantasizing in prayer. Don't let this term startle you because Webster says fantasize means "to develop imaginative and often fantastic views or ideas." And you'll never have greater or more fantastic ideas than those God has for you and is waiting to do through you (Luke 10:19, Eph. 3:20, Phil. 4:13).

On the basis of this definition and these Scripture

verses, think about what you might want to be, be doing,
or have accomplished *five years* from now. Write
down a description of those goals. Now what goals must
you accomplish this year to feed into the five-year goals?
The "Life Purpose" chart that follows can be a valuable
tool in your own goal-setting. Either by using the
one in the book or by making a larger copy for a
worksheet, you will find that this chart will help you
visually as you do the exercise.

LIFE PURPOSE

Be doing in fifteen years	Have accomplished in fifteen years

Five-year goals

One-year goals

Immediate Steps

The lines on the lower part of the chart are for listing immediate steps needed to reach your one-year goals. You may be wondering if one-year goals are necessary, because you believe you know what you want and that you will act accordingly. However, my experience has shown me that most people are not consciously aware of their goals or even of the many decisions they make.

Think about ones you've already made today: the time you got up; the clothes you chose to wear; the book you selected to read to your child; the store where you shopped, etc. All of us need to raise our level of awareness concerning all the decisions we make, so that when we make a decision we will be proud of it. For— regardless of what we sometimes think—we do have control over most of our decisions. This means we can set goals if we decide to. And this brings in the importance of the will.

The Scriptures make it clear that God expects us to control ourselves through our wills instead of allowing our feelings and emotions to control us. Oswald Chambers said, "Will is the essential element in God's creation of man. The will is the whole man active. I cannot give up my will, I must exercise it. The battle is lost or won in the secret places of the will before God."

David was called a man after God's own heart, and in the Psalms we have multitudes of examples of David saying *"I will." "I will* bless the Lord . . . *I will* abide . . . *I will* trust . . . *I will* sing . . . *I will* give thanks . . . *I will* take heed to my ways . . . *I will* keep my mouth with a bridle. . . ." Once we have determined—like David —to say *I will,* then we simply move on to *how.*

To best determine the steps necessary to reach a goal, it is helpful to take a piece of paper and make five columns. Title the first column Goal; the second, Present Situation; the third, Forces Helping; the fourth, Forces Hindering; the fifth, Steps to Goal. Now let's fill in the columns with a sample goal.

Column 1: *To read twenty books this year.*

Column 2: *Last year read eight and a half.*

Column 3: *Personal need for more knowledge in certain*

*areas; desire to be able to converse about current
literature; to give a boost to my self-esteem.*
Column 4: *The demands of the children; no specific
reading program; TV; newspapers; magazines.*
Column 5: *Decide on books; estimate total number of
pages, times my reading speed, to "guesstimate"
approximate amount of time needed; decide how to find
blocks of reading time free from the children; confine
most of my magazine reading to waiting periods in offices;
do not duplicate my awareness of the news through TV
and newspapers (do one or the other).*

Making this five-column layout will enable you to tailor
your steps in the fifth column in such a way that they
focus directly on overcoming forces that have hindered
you in the past.

Another means of insuring success is to concentrate
on a few goals at a time by prioritizing them. One way to
do this is suggested below:

PRIORITIZING WORKSHEET

	Priority	
List eight of your goals.	**1**	**2**
1. _____	_____	
2. _____	_____	
3. _____	_____	
4. _____	_____	
5. _____	_____	
6. _____	_____	
7. _____	_____	
8. _____	_____	

For each one, decide whether for you this is an A, B, or
C. Write in first column.

A = Very important
B = Somewhat important
C = Not so important

If you have more than one A—use second column to
number 1, 2, or 3 priority.

PLANNING SHEETS

One of the most frequent complaints I hear from mothers is, "I don't feel as though I accomplished anything today or this week. I was busy all the time but I don't know what I did. It makes me feel that I'm not doing anything constructive or anything with long-range results." Such a feeling can be eliminated if you develop a written system. The system or plan has to be kept simple or it won't work. Of course, simple is an arbitrary term and what is simple for one may be complex for another. So I'll offer several suggestions; choose the ones which will work best for you.

When I had several preschoolers, each evening I made a practice of writing down a list of things I had to do the following day. Then I'd prioritize them by doing the most unpleasant first and the most pleasant last. The value of such a habit is that—even amidst the multitudinous interruptions of small children—my day became more enjoyable as it went along. As a result, I found that I got much more accomplished, because I saved the enjoyable things to do last. I found that this system also helped eliminate procrastination.

A friend of mine always wrote on her evening list the five most important things she had to do the next day, in order of their importance. Then the next day she'd start working on the most important things and progress down the list. Many days she did not get completely through her list, but she didn't feel concerned or pressured by that fact, because she had the satisfaction of knowing that she was always working on what was most important.

As my children reached school age and the scope of our lives became more complex, I began making out a Weekly Planning Sheet on which I included such items as: Letters to Write, People to See, Things to Be Done, Things to Be Planned, Phone Calls to Make. Under each category I drew enough lines to include all that I could think of during my planning time, plus some extra ones for forgotten or unexpected items. For the phone calls, I took time to write the person's number beside his name. This saved the repeated time and effort of looking up the number again if the person was not available the first time I'd call. Another time-saver for me was the act of printing largely all the headings and spaces (see below):

WEEKLY PLANNING SHEET

Date _____

Letters to write

_____   _____   (The short line is to
_____   _____   number according
_____   _____   to priority.)

_____   _____

People to see

_____   _____

_____   _____

_____   _____

Then after listing all categories in this manner, I took this paper to the printer and had him make fifty-two copies, enough for one a week throughout the year. This greatly helped expedite my planning time. When you do this, remember to be realistic in your planning, being sure to allow adequate time for each task, plus additional time for interruptions.

An excellent book for every Christian woman, that will also help her plan her time, is *Disciplines of the Beautiful Woman,* by Anne Ortlund (Word Books, Waco, Texas).

MOTHER SAVERS

Most of us go about our daily tasks in a nonthinking, habitual way. We do something this way because our mother before us did it this way, or because it seemed easier once, or because we always have and we don't want to take time to try a different way. Few of us take time to evaluate our tasks periodically to see if there might be a more efficient way of doing something. As I checked into the whole efficiency idea myself, I learned that there are more efficient ways to do some of the tasks I had always done one way. Some of the following thoughts may begin to prime your "efficiency computer" and help you come up with new ideas of your own.

Keep quick emergency meals in your pantry and freezer for unexpected guests, including children, and for days when the unexpected occurs. Make your own TV dinners on three-sectioned TV trays by using up leftovers that are so small they would probably be thrown away. These can be frozen and then warmed up for an occasional buffet dinner night when everyone has an individual menu.

Label everything. Whether you write labels by hand or use a gadget, labeling will help organize your home. Make labels with important phone numbers and stick them onto the phone. Label linen closet shelves, indicating where the various sheet sizes go. Write plant names on labels and stick them on the pots; add the kind of fertilizer and how often it should be used, as well as the frequency of watering. Label right shoes for the very young. Label towel racks. Label boots, mittens, and scarves.

Keep a stock of already-wrapped gifts on hand. Have birthday gifts, hostess gifts, presents for confined friends (both children and adults), and gifts for those times when a "just because" remembrance is appropriate. Be sure to have on hand a stock of all-occasion cards.

Train the whole family to use the washing machine as the hamper for white clothes and a bathroom hamper for colored clothes. Thus, when the washer is filled, you can run it without having to sort. A third hamper for drycleaning eliminates roundup time and the possibility of forgetting something the day you go to the cleaners.

Place a hook for each child at a height where he can reach it and enforce the hanging up of coats and sweaters for even the youngest child. Avoid like the plague a box for everybody's boots and a drawer for everybody's gloves.

When emptying the dishwasher or the drainer, set the table for the next meal. Add to your lists of children's tasks the setting of the breakfast table the night before.

Hang a calendar "For Family Appointments Only" near a telephone. This will alleviate appointment conflicts that take you and your children in opposite directions on the same afternoon.

Sometime during the weekend, organize your child's outfits for each day of the coming week. Put them on separate hangers marked for the appropriate day, or place total outfits together, allowing the child to choose one for each day.

CO-OP GOAL-SETTING

People are motivated by their own goals and this includes children. So if you want your child to attain goals, you must allow him to plan his own steps for achieving them. For example, my neighbor's three-year-old daughter never seemed to be able to find her shoes. Many times members of the family would be late for appointments because they were looking for Sara's shoes

To solve this problem, Sara's mother printed the word "Goal" at the top of a large sheet of paper. Below that she printed, "Always Know Where Sara's Shoes Are," with the picture of a woman and a little girl looking at a pair of shoes. Beneath the picture she printed the target date and drew a large red heart (the goal was being written the week before Valentine's Day).

Lower down on the paper she printed the words "This Is How." When she had completed the goal-setting paper the mother sat down with Sara and discussed it with her. The girl immediately ran and got one of her plastic shopping bags (one of her favorite "toys" of the moment She hung the bag on her bedroom door and told her mother, "Every time I take off my shoes I'll put them in this bag."

My neighbor told me the positive results were immediate and the lost shoes problem was soon completely solved. Why? Sara was proud of the fac was *her* own idea.

The thing to remember in goal-planning with children is that they might come up with some very different steps for achieving the goal than the ones you would choose. When this happens, you must remember that the purpose is to reach the goal, not necessarily to use your steps. Children are often more highly motivated by the incorporation of their ideas in the solving of a problem. And they are further motivated by their own implementation of those ideas.

One of my college instructors made goal-setting contracts for her children when they were school age. She made up a sheet of paper with Goal-Setting Contract printed across the top. Below this she printed: "We plan to accomplish this (leaving several lines) by this date____ : I plan to take these steps (several more lines). These people are responsible for (several more lines)." She photocopied the forms to make them seem more like a professional contract.

One of her "contracts," which was made between her and her son Phillip, was set up as follows:

GOAL-SETTING CONTRACT

We plan to accomplish this:

To learn the multiplication tables through 10.

_____

_____

_____

by this date: October 15

I plan to take these steps:

To make multiplication table cards.

To study them ½ hour each day.

To write 1/10 of them down each day.

_____

_____

These people are responsible for:

Mother to furnish material for cards and help make them

if necessary.

Mother to quiz Phillip fifteen minutes a day.

_____

_____

_____

Signed:

Phillip: _____

Others: (In this case it was mother.)

_____

_____

Teaching a child this kind of goal-setting early in his life establishes the habitual process of self-motivation. And, by establishing and recording the names of the persons to be involved in the process, along with the extent of their involvement, you automatically eliminate the usual blame-passing excuses.

TIME PATTERNS

God in his creative wisdom designed time patterns for us, day and night. Then he instructed us to "redeem the time"—to use it wisely. One means of helping preschool children to understand how they can best use their daily time is to draw a "Pie of Life." Draw a large circle to represent a twenty-four-hour period. Now draw slices in your pie to represent proportionately the amount of time each day your child spends on each category.

For example: Sleep would be a slice equal to approximately 1/3 or more of the pie. Other categories you can list are: doing chores, playing alone, playing with friends, eating, reading, etc. If you choose to, you can draw pictures representative of each category in the various slices. Such a visual is an excellent tool to help your child comprehend his total day.

Older children not only like to draw their present "Pie of Life," but also to draw what they consider the proper size each slice should be. By allowing them to do this you give them another opportunity to help establish their own goals. Ask them what they consider the ideal sizes of some of the slices as compared with the present sizes. You can then discuss some steps that would make their real pie-of-life more like their ideal pie-of-life.

FAITH IS NEVER SURPRISED BY SUCCESS

"Have two goals: wisdom—that is, knowing and doing right—and common sense. Don't let them slip away, for they fill you with living energy, and are a feather in your cap. They keep you safe from defeat and disaster and from stumbling off the trail" (Prov. 3:21-23, TLB).

Plan your goals. Talk to God about them. They are your statement of faith concerning what God wants you to be and to do. "We should make plans—counting on God to direct us."

ELEVEN
OUTSIDE INVOLVEMENT: WHAT, WHEN, AND WHY

Everywhere I go, I hear the same desire from mothers:
They want their lives to count. They dread the possibility
that their lives might be insipid or ineffective. They
long for a challenge big enough to demand their
allegiance, exciting enough to rally their enthusiasm, and
vital enough to warrant their time.

A mother's problem is not whether she should assume
responsibilities beyond the home. The problem is
how *many* responsibilities. How well I know that the
multiple roles of "mother" can make a virtual seesaw
of any woman's life. On the one hand, family obligations
always weigh heavily; while on the other hand, other
involvements continually vie for priority time.

Personal fulfillment comes when you have the inner
assurance that you have spent your God-given time and
energies wisely—in relation to your family's needs, the
needs of the world outside your home, and the cry of
your inner self.

The previous chapter was aimed at helping you to use
your time wisely. This one is focused on increasing your
awareness of the opportunities and responsibilities that
surround you. In order to gain the greatest fulfillment
in our mothering, we must look for and respond to
opportunities for using our particular skills and interests in

other settings. I am woefully aware that we all too
often respond to the lure of outside involvement based on
the weak ploy, "Someone must do it," or, "But *you* already
know how." But how much more satisfying and
completing it is if we complement our mothering by
developing and using a new ability.

When she is involved to some degree in outside
interests, a mother will better withstand the temptation to
smother her child, and may insure his more wholesome
adjustment than if she devoted her total energies to him.
Children can benefit enormously from having an involved
—rather than totally self-involved—mother. The more
fulfilled a mother's own life is, the less need she'll
have for her child to fill it for her. Sociologist Pauline
Bart of the University of Illinois Medical Center found, in
a study of depressed middle-aged mothers, that the typical
patients were ones who had depended upon their children
to make life meaningful for them.

The feeling of "not having enough time" for being a
mother—to say nothing of being involved outside
the home—sometimes comes from a frustrating lack of
self-satisfaction and fulfillment. One of the best remedies
for such a stultifying impasse is to grow a little every
day (improve yourself), and to accomplish a portion of a
long-range goal.

DO YOU HAVE A HOBBY?

A hobby will give you a new enthusiasm and make you
a more interesting person. It will bring new people
into your life and help guard against loneliness when your
children are grown.

A friend of mine who did a lot of sewing realized one
day that she had accumulated several jars of loose
buttons. She decided to get some books from the library
and read about buttons. It was the beginning of a
fascinating hobby. Lynn now has hundreds of valuable
buttons mounted on boards. She is not a public speaker
per se, but is often asked to talk to groups about her
buttons. This simple hobby has boosted her self-esteem,

increased her children's pride in her, and given her many opportunities to share Christ.

My hobby is writing. When my children were tiny, I would sometimes trade an afternoon of baby-sitting with a friend who was an avid golfer. Both of us now use our hobbies for earning extra money. Charlotte teaches golf to elementary school children and I write for publication.

Consider taking a class at your community college, either academic or for sheer enrichment. Learn cake decorating, the art of movie critiquing, accounting—the options are endless. Take a class on teaching tips, then get into the Word of God and teach a Bible study class. Take a class in literature, then hold a book discussion group in your home and share what you've learned.

One mother I know belongs to a group they call SPA (Spiritual/Physical Activity). They meet weekly for Bible study and exercises. Each mother takes a turn baby-sitting for the group, so that child care does not become a financial drain for anyone. Some cities now have a homework hotline which consists of a group of mothers who were formerly teachers. They spend a specific time at the library answering questions from students who are experiencing difficulties with their homework. Some cities even pay for this service.

If earning money is one of your desires, there are many creative ways to do this at home. Sally designs and sells crewel kits to local department stores. Polly teaches craft courses in her home. Harriet put her secretarial training to work. She became a stenographer to small businesses and clubs unable to afford their own secretaries. She sets her own hours and work load. Every time Diane makes a dress for her daughter, she makes two—cutting them out at the same time—then sells one.

Frances loves to bake. One day a week she bakes several kinds of bakery goods. Since she lives only two blocks from a factory, she can sell her baked goods to the factory workers as they leave the plant. Ruth delivers "Meals-on-Wheels" one day a week, accompanied by her little boy. They both benefit: She acquires extra money, he acquires many additional "Grandmas" and "Grandpas."

Involving yourself can improve yourself, which helps to create a pride in yourself. And you must be proud of yourself before your child can be proud of you. Don't push your own needs aside to live the role of a giving-only-to-my-child mother. In order to give freely to your child, you must have something to give. By seeking a happy balance between homemaking and meaningful involvements beyond the home, you will find yourself giving to your child—not just a better home environment —but an improved total environment.

SCHOOLS BELONG TO YOU

My perspective on the educational system comes from having been actively involved: as a mother, as an elected school board member, as a teacher, as the public relations director for a state School Board Association and a public affairs officer for a state Department of Education. My participation in the American school system has impressed upon me a serious lack of involvement on the part of parents. The American school system is grounded in the belief that parents should control the education of their children. But because of parental apathy, this control is being lost. As one who speaks from experience, I urge you mothers to get involved, even before your child goes to school, if possible. But whenever you do it, do so knowledgeably.

Do you know the members of your local school board? Is there at least one member who represents the Christian viewpoint? If not, there should be. If it isn't feasible for you to run for office at this time, then it is your responsibility to help elect another *qualified* Christian.

Attend the school board meetings. Other special interest groups do, and as a mother you cannot prevent corruption of your school system if you don't know what is being said and done at the school board meetings. However, before you go, do your homework so you will know why you are for or against an issue.

While I was serving on the school board, a teacher decided to involve the students in a piece of literature that was basically unacceptable to the Christian community. One student took the play home to show his mother. She read it, called her pastor, and began alerting other parents. At the next school board meeting we had a packed house. One by one people would step to the microphone to give a highly emotional barrage of words against the play.

As the meeting began to reach a feverish pitch, the board asked for a show of hands from the people who had read the play. There were only five, and two of those were the teacher and myself. Immediately, the whole crowd lost its credibility with the board and the board tabled the issue. So I repeat, get involved, but do it knowledgeably.

Read textbooks. School boards make the final decision on the textbooks that go into your classrooms. Ask your board to appoint a textbook selection committee with a cross section of community members serving on it. Offer to be a part of it. Ask that the favored textbooks be put on display in the school for any community member to peruse before the board votes to purchase them. Then make sure that you gather up some other mothers to go look at them. In my school district, during the two weeks the books were on display, it was rare when more than nine or ten parents came to read them. This negligence on the part of God's people is producing a crop of pernicious literature in classrooms across our country.

Know policies concerning the content of school textbooks. Does either your local school board or your state board of education have one? Why or why not? It is essential that you know this in order to protect your child from being taught from books that are contrary to biblical principles.

Does your state have a bill to protect parents' rights in school matters? Why or why not? This type of bill can speak to such questions as: The rights of parents to review all school instructional and examination materials. The rights of parental consent prior to: psychological testing of your child, personal counseling of your child, participation by your child in a sensitivity training group or his assignment to any innovative program. Such a bill can also speak to the rights of parents to disallow any person in the public school to act as a "change agent" toward any of their child's attitudes, values, and religious or political beliefs.

Give some assisting time. Ask your school board to use or hire mothers as instructional aides. Mothers can listen to children read, play skill games, help in the library, make instructional materials for teachers, supervise the painting center, etc. Mothers with particular talents can conduct the school chorus, start a school newspaper, teach sewing or languages.

If no such program materializes you can still offer to help in some way—as a room mother, in the lunchroom, and of course, in your PTA (or whatever your parent-teacher group is called). If your school doesn't have a parent-teacher group, take the initiative and start one.

In one of our school districts, a mother who was disgruntled with the report cards being used decided to spend some time collecting report cards from schools all over the nation. From all her samples, she designed a two-way report card that she presented to the school board for consideration. The school board was unanimous in its acceptance and adoption of the cards.

So now the cards that go home in that district have a written report from the teacher, with space for the parent to respond as well as two questions for the parent to answer: (1) "What observations of your child in his home environment have you made that might be useful to us?" (2) "What reactions to school activities have you observed which might be significant to us?"

At a later school board meeting a teacher shared this outcome from one mother's response to the new report cards. "Pam was the youngest of six girls. She was having difficulties in school by overasserting herself. On this new card her mother felt encouraged to tell about Pam's being the youngest child and to suggest that since she was a particularly fine reader, it might be helpful for Pam to assist a group of younger children in their reading."

The teacher appreciated the mother's insight and her suggestion. As a result, Pam was given the opportunity to do as suggested. The result: She became part of a situation in which she was not only the oldest of a group, but was also able to do things the others could not do. The teacher stated with satisfaction, "Pam's aggressive assertiveness has ceased."

Another example of one mother's involvement making a difference.

Know what is happening in your child's school. You have spent the first six years of your child's life carefully building a foundation. The school will spend the next twelve years building upon your foundation. It's up to you to know what they propose to build and then to participate in it.

YOU CAN MAKE A DIFFERENCE

Write letters to the editor of the local newspaper, pointing out problem areas and suggesting solutions. Newspapers that carry pornographic ads will respond to a letter deluge and subscription cancellations.

Attend zoning meetings and voice your protests when the location of an undesirable business is to be decided. If a store is putting sensual material on its open magazine racks, you should take a group to meet with the owner. If he doesn't remove the material from the open racks, then picket in front of his store.

God's Word tells us we are *not* to sit idly by and let the smut merchants peddle their wares without opposition. "Blessed—happy, fortunate, prosperous and enviable—is the man who walks and lives not in the counsel of the ungodly (following their advice, their plans and purposes), nor stands (submissive and inactive) in the path where sinners walk . . ." (Psa. 1:1, AB). When we neglect to do what we can to support high standards and clean literature, then we will be "standing submissive and inactive" in the sinners' pathway.

Another influential ware peddler is the television. In the United States, over six million preschoolers watch TV several hours daily. By the time a child reaches kindergarten he has spent more time in front of the TV (between 15,000 and 20,000 hours), than the average student has spent in classes during four years of college. It is important to remember that these early years are the time when a child is forming his informational and self-concept categories which will guide him for the rest of his life. At the time that this book is being written, several surveys have indicated that over 78 percent of American families use the TV as a baby-sitter, which indicates that all of this watching is largely unsupervised.

What is the child watching? First, he is being immersed in the culture's values through commercials. Children's programs, for example, average 20 per hour. The child is encouraged to cajole his parents into acquiring the product. Peer norms are established, and if he doesn't have or soon acquire the latest TV toy—he's out!

Simply because they see or hear something frequently, children begin assuming that it is true. This phenomenon applies also to adults and is known to social psychologists as "saturation." This means that it matters not how ridiculous a statement is, if it's repeated often enough, a certain percentage of people will believe it. And the percentage is greater among children.

When we realize that children use the information they watch on TV to help construct their concept of who they are and want to become, it should cause us to be very selective in what we allow them to take in. It seems rather significant that Elton Rule, president of ABC, Inc., allows his seven-year-old daughter to watch only one hour of TV a day.

The Bible speaks very directly about the power of the eye to control the whole person. "The light of the body is the eye: therefore when thine eye is single, thy whole body also is full of light; but when thine eye is evil, thy body also is full of darkness. Take heed therefore that the light which is in thee be not darkness" (Luke 11:34, 35).

Writing letters is a meaningful way to influence TV programming. Every mother can write a personal letter of protest to the network, producer, and commercial sponsor of every morally, spiritually, and intellectually degrading program that she's aware of. As Christian mothers, we sometimes are concerned about the first two of these, but fail to recognize the importance of the third. We should also protest the fact that the majority of recent popular television shows have to do with the antics of essentially dumb people. Most of these shows are on the air while even young children are awake. This means that if we allow our children to watch such programs, they will be exposed to: glorification of illiteracy, lawbreaking, and recklessness, with all their deadly stereotyping.

If every mother who has a concern for the proper nurturing of her child's mind would write these letters— as well as letters of thanks and appreciation for positive programs—TV programming would be changed. In the words of William Paley, chairman of the CBS Board, "We make money giving people what they want, so what they are getting is apparently what they want." Let him know what *you* want.

Who controls the "off" knob on your TV? Another important step in controlling your child's TV tastes and appetite is for *you* to control *your own* personal TV tastes and appetite. You can begin by monitoring your own television viewing time and habits. Keep a chart for a month, adding up the time you spend watching TV and nothing the kinds of programs you choose. Do the same for your children.

With this information at hand, you will soon detect a pattern and begin to develop a clearer idea of how TV affects the lives of your family. Does TV dictate meal-times and bedtimes? Does watching TV reduce the time you have for reading, writing letters, talking with friends and family, or getting involved in community activities?

One way to help discipline your TV habits is to make a checklist by which you evaluate the TV programs you and your child watch. In order to make the most accurate judgment about the programs, you'll have to view them for several successive airings.

The checklist I found most helpful asked the following questions:

(1) Is watching this program responsible Christian stewardship? "So then every one of us shall give account of himself to God" (Rom. 14:12).

(2) Is this program informative or entertaining? If informative, does it offer the best medium for my child to receive this information? "Take heed therefore how you hear" (Luke 8:18). If entertaining, is there anything about this entertainment that is contrary to God's Word? ". . . let it not be once named among you, as becometh saints; neither filthiness, nor foolish talking, nor jesting, which are not [fitting]" (Eph. 5:3, 4).

(3) Will watching this program contribute in a positive way to my child's growth? "Do not be conformed to this world—this age, fashioned after and adapted to its external, superficial customs. But be transformed (changed) by the [entire] renewal of your mind—by its new ideals and its new attitude—so that you may prove [for yourselves] what is the good and acceptable and perfect will of God" (Rom. 12:2, AB).

Contact the following sources for TV monitoring information:

Action for Children's Television, 46 Austin St., Newtonville, MA 02160. This organization provides information concerning what to watch for and work for in children's TV, including advice on how to talk about, look at, and choose programs with your child.

The PTA TV Action Center, 700 North Rush St., Chicago, IL 60611, will provide you with information about a campaign to reduce violence in television programs among other things.

The TV Action Center has a national toll-free hotline number: 800-323-5177 (Illinois residents can call 800-942-4266). This center will answer any of your questions about the TV industry and can put you in touch with community groups that are involved in improving TV programming.

Others influenced by your letters are your congressmen.
Write to your representative or senator, urging him to
vote or not to vote for some pending legislation. Ask to be
put on mailing lists. Sending petitions is not the same
thing as writing a letter. Elected officials aren't moved by
petitions. But they do get interested when they receive
a personal letter, even if it's only a couple of paragraphs.
Letters are influential! And the most effective ones
include information about your sphere of influence. An
example might be:

*Dear Senator Smith: In talking with my PTA group [or
twelve women in our mothers' group; or at our precinct
meeting, or whatever the group may be], one of the
women said she heard a rumor that you were going to vote
for Bill Number _____. Because our group believes
the bill will have a detrimental effect on our children,
the group unanimously agreed that if you vote for the bill,
we will form a coalition with other groups in behalf of
someone else at the next election. Therefore, I was asked
to write to you so that you could verify or deny the rumor.*

You can be assured that such a letter will merit a
thoughtful response. The elected official realizes that
probably as few as half of 1 percent of the people exert
the control that governs our country. So when the "voluble
minority" speaks, the politicians listen. You can be
one of the citizens they respond to.
Are you helping to control your country by voting? Are
you registered to vote? Are your neighbors, your Christian
friends, your fellow church members? It is estimated
that there are at least fifteen million biblically oriented
Christians in this country who are not registered to vote.
That's enough votes to change presidential elections and
control the Congress and other levels of offices. You can
help make this difference by volunteering to be a deputy
registrar; then register as many concerned, responsible
people as possible.
Be a precinct worker. Your county elections board can
tell you how. "Precinct" has a rather ominous sound
for some of us, but it shouldn't. The precinct is the

foundation of the political organization. Actually, it is in the precinct that elections are won or lost—including local, state, and national. And yet a precinct is simply a neighborhood with a precinct leader and a number of precinct workers. Precinct workers canvass the neighborhood in person or by telephone to determine the location and viewpoint of their party members. They make an effort to get their neighbors registered; they recruit workers. At election time they—together with other volunteers they have recruited—locate voters who are in favor of their candidate and those who can be persuaded to vote for their candidate. On election day they assist voters who favor their candidate, in getting to the polls. The same procedure wins elections for candidates of: the school board, the city council, the state senate, the U.S. Congress and the Presidency. And since precinct elections are sometimes won or lost by as small as a one-vote margin, *even your vote* can make a difference.

Either run for office or help someone else be elected. Urge concerned Christians in your community to get involved in the precincts. When enough believers become precinct workers, they can elect responsible people to leadership positions and clean up the country from within. It takes only twenty-five to fifty precinct workers to put any man or woman in or out of the state legislature.

Who are your city council members? Do you know any of them? You should, because they are important to you. They make the decisions that allow or disallow a porno shop to be located in your city. Who is your county commissioner? He controls your police department. Your governor determines who runs the state penal institutions. Who are your wardens or superintendents for jails and prisons? Your tax dollars are paying their salaries. The people in those key positions will determine whether born-again chaplains are hired to minister to inmates.

Start a political action group. Make each person in the group responsible for a newly introduced bill. Examine it for negative or positive overtones; explain it to the group and get their opinion. Then make each person responsible for a letter-writing and followup campaign on that particular bill.

There isn't a mother anywhere who cannot contribute *something*. Involve your children in politics. They love to go door to door handing out literature. They're great at stuffing, licking, and stamping envelopes. Make provisions for them to meet the candidates. Candidates will almost always take time to talk with a child. Let your child watch election returns. Personal involvement is the best way for any child to learn "civics."

Be informed. Some publications that can help are:

Human Events
422 First St. S.E.
Washington, DC 20003

Intercessors for America Prayer Newsletter
P.O. Box D
Elyria, OH 40035

The Bible gives us many examples of women who used their God-given creativity to meet the challenges around them, and to improve the world in which they lived. Abigail listened to God, chose involvement, and changed the course of an army. Esther stood up for right when wrong was popular. Because she chose involvement she saved many people from a violent death.

Even back in the mountains of Ephraim, there was a woman with a strong faith in a living God. Her name was Deborah. She is referred to as a "mother in Israel," a title—in my opinion—that's perhaps the finest that can be applied to any woman. But Deborah was more than a mother. Even in those difficult days, she didn't become so absorbed in the needs of her own family that she had no interests outside her own domestic problems. She cared for the welfare of those around her. She also took notice of the affairs of the nation, so that she was able to develop an informed opinion on national policy and to give advice on both minor and weighty problems.

It is nothing but idle talk (which Scripture condemns in 2 Timothy 2:16, AB), if you are deploring the state of affairs, criticizing the President and our government, making shocked comments concerning low community morals—unless you are involved in doing something about the situation.

To say that you can do nothing is inexcusable. History frequently records thrilling sagas of how a single woman has altered the course of events. But in each case—whatever the circumstances—the woman who made the difference was an informed woman. And that made her involvement worthwhile.

TWELVE
LIVING THE WORD

Hanging above my desk is a plaque which reads: "There are only two lasting bequests we can give our children —one is roots, the other wings." Experience has taught me that if we neglect to give the first, we will be incapable of giving the second. Roots are the foundation of security from which a child develops his wings.

One translation of Psalm 91:1 says, "He who dwells in the secret place of the Most High shall remain stable and fixed under the shadow of the Almighty. [Whose power no foe can withstand]" (AB). That means anyone whose life is firmly fixed beneath God's shadow ("under his wings," KJV), will no longer be conquered by the frustrations that surround him. That person will be the conqueror.

Now, we can be in someone's shadow only if we are close enough to him to hear what he is saying to us. And we can dwell in the shadow of Almighty God only when we continually dwell on his Word. How can we do that? Here's how God answers the question: "You shall lay up these My words in your [mind and] heart and in your [entire] being" (Deut. 11:18, AB). A busy mother wonders, "How is this possible? The children are always underfoot." God's answer continues . . .

"Tie his words to your hand to remind you to obey them.

Tie them to your forehead between your eyes.
Teach them to your children.
Talk about them when you are sitting at home . . .
When you are out walking . . .
At bedtime and before breakfast.
Write them upon the doors of your houses."
It sounds all-inclusive, doesn't it? We are to keep God's
words before us at all times. And on top of that, God
is telling us to "Teach them [his words] to our children."

God knows what he is talking about, because even
very young children can begin memorizing Scriptures.
The best time to plan their memorizing is as soon as
they are old enough to string words together in sentences.
Of course, for these very young children you will
at first give them only parts of verses or short phrases.

Teach God's Word to them in a positive manner. Too
often some parents use Scripture on their children as a
"scare tactic." This can be devastating to a child. One
such child, about five or six years old, was in my Sunday
school class. She was terrified of God.

Not until I learned some of the Scripture verses she
had been taught—along with her mother's amplification of
them—did I learn the reason for her fear. This little
girl was taught the portion of a verse that said, "Thou God
seest me" (Gen. 16:13).

The mother's interpretation to her child was: "God is
spying on you. God sees you when you're naughty.
Remember, wherever you are, even if your mother is not
with you, God sees you, and he will punish you if you
are naughty."

How much better for that child, or any child, if the
interpretation of that verse had been something like this:
"God loves you and cares about you. He sees you and
is watching over you." We mothers possess the awesome
power of being able to introduce our children to the
Lord as one who loves them. When the child has learned
to know God as a loving authority figure, he will more
willingly submit to words of correction.

One of the verses I have "discovered" that is special for
young children is Psalm 92:1: "It is good to say, 'Thank

you' to the Lord" (TLB). After you have helped your child to internalize the first part of this verse, you can later teach him the rest: "And every evening rejoice in all his faithfulness."

When your child has learned the concept of being a helper, Psalm 54:4, "God is my helper," will be meaningful. The rest of the verse goes on to say, "He is a friend of mine!" One of my young sons did not want to fear anything, so Psalm 31:24 became a favorite of his: Take courage if you are depending on the Lord" (TLB). Another verse from Psalms that encouraged one of my approaching-school-age children was, "[God] fills me with strength and protects me wherever I go" (Psa. 18:32, TLB).

When selecting Scripture verses for your child, it doesn't really matter which translation you choose, because there are several good ones. Some mothers have found *The Living Bible* to be an easier version for a very young child to understand. The translation is not nearly as important as is your thoughtful, prayerful searching of the Scripture to locate words that are meaningful to and for your child.

There is no one better equipped than you, the mother, to help your child learn the words of God that will become increasingly meaningful to him throughout his life. For that reason we must take care, lest we get so caught up in what we think they "ought" to learn, that we neglect to teach them what they "need" to know for their own well-being.

The Psalms are full of praises and your child should learn as many praise verses from them as possible. Is there any better way for your child to begin a relationship with God than through the quoting of words of praise? The book of Proverbs too, is an excellent "primer" in learning to know God.

TALK ABOUT THEM

Remember, these Scripture verses will be retained only if they are repeated over and over again. As a mother

you must learn to use every moment available to impress
a verse on your child's mind: while buttoning sweaters,
drawing bath water, eating meals. I used to put verses on
the refrigerator at the child's level. And even though
a preschooler couldn't read them, he felt important.
"Mother put 'my verse' where I can read it!" Of course
my verse was at my own eye level. So every time we
went to the refrigerator each of us could read our verses
aloud.

Another excellent means of teaching Scripture is with a
tape recorder. Children will love hearing your voice
repeating the verses for them, and they will quickly learn
to repeat them with you.

WRITE THEM UPON THE DOORS

Of course, when your child is old enough to print, he
can write his own verses on cards or posters for
memorizing.

God initiated this practice a long, long time ago when
he instructed Israel's kings to write for themselves
"a book, the copy of the law" and then read it all the days
of their lives (Deut. 17:18-20). God commanded this
because he knew how important it was for one to actually
write the words himself, so that they would be impressed
upon his memory.

My children and I taped Scripture verses on mirrors,
bedposts, bulletin boards, and even the dashboard of our
car. We literally kept the Word of God before our eyes
constantly.

Recently I saw a rather unique memorizing aid in a
Christian bookstore. It consisted of a leather bracelet like
a watchband with a changeable Scripture verse in a
clear window instead of a watch face. Such an item is
excellent for memorizing Scripture.

Whichever method you use, memorizing God's Word
requires repetition. Read the verses aloud to your child
and yourself again and again. Soon you will be pleased
to hear him repeating them verbatim. The verses you
choose for yourself may not be the same ones you choose

for him. However, with your help the child will quickly
assimilate into his very being both God's words and his
life principles.

Scripture memorization for young children need not
be drudgery. We have already established that children
love to learn. Children also love to do what they see
their parents doing. So the practice of imprinting God's
words in his heart will become difficult and unpleasant
for your child only if you allow it to become difficult
and unpleasant for yourself.

In memorizing Scripture, you are simply obeying
God's commands: "These words, which I am commanding
you this day, shall be [first] in your own mind and heart;
[then] you shall whet and sharpen them, so as to make
them penetrate, and teach and impress them diligently
upon the [minds and] hearts of your children" (Deut.
6:7, AB). For me this passage says that as my child grows,
it is my responsibility as a mother to feed him the Word
in an effective manner. I believe the best way to do this
is to make his learning personal—and enjoyable.

This personal introduction to the Scriptures can be
accomplished through the use of the "Truth *and*
Consequences" looseleaf booklet I have developed. Or, if
you like, you can produce an adequate substitute yourself.

To do this, use a small 3" x 5" recipe file box or a
small loose leaf notebook. A promise from God's Word
should be hand-printed or typed on the page, such as:
"For [God] orders his angels to protect you wherever
you go" (Psa. 91:11). For a preschooler you would
draw angels protecting children.

Then, either above or below the promise, write the
"condition" for the promise. For the example given above,
the condition would be: "He who dwells in the secret
place of the Most High." You can explain that this actually
means living in a continuous relationship, talking with
God in prayer, as he speaks to us through his Word. And
only when we meet this "condition" do we have the right
to claim his promise. For the preschooler, you could use
a picture of a child with a Bible in front of him, looking
up into heaven as if talking to someone.

Another "truth *and* consequence" concept is found in
Philippians 4:4 (TLB): "Always be full of joy in the Lord;
I say it again, rejoice!" This truth can be illustrated
by a child giving thanks to God.

The consequence of this behavior is stated in verse 7:
"If you do this you will experience God's peace. . . . His
peace will keep your thoughts and your hearts quiet and
at rest" (to be illustrated by a happy child).

It is vital that the condition for each promise be clearly
understood by the child, because comprehension of the
"truth/consequence" principle will make a difference in
the way he prays and lives.

Jesus said he came to give us life more abundantly. The
promises throughout his Word describe the more
abundant life. These promises are from God for us—*today*.
Since Jesus Christ is the same yesterday, today, and
forever, God will always do what he has said. "God is not
a man, that he should lie; he doesn't change his mind
like we humans do. Has he ever promised without doing
what he said?" (Num. 23:19, TLB).

When we begin to internalize such magnificent truths, it
becomes an exciting adventure for us as we watch God
keep his promises and perform his miracles in our lives.
But when we read these promises, and teach them to our
children without including the condition for the promise,
we are neither learning nor teaching them correctly.
The result can only be discouragement when (through our
fatal omission) it appears that God is not keeping his
promises.

Remember: The promises are there. God both gives
them and keeps them. But failure to realize and act on
this principle, Jesus said, "is caused by your ignorance
of the Scriptures and of God's power!" (Matt. 22:29,
TLB). The error is multiplied if we, because of ignorance,
do not know and teach the daily, personal, miraculous
power of God.

I remember how excited I became the day I discovered
the fact that God has a vested interest in both the truth
and the consequences of his Word. "I am alert and active,"
he says, "watching over My word to perform it" (Jer.
1:12, AB).

AT BEDTIME AND BEFORE BREAKFAST

Another method of memorizing Scripture is to incorporate it into your daily devotions. This really worked with my children. I would occasionally choose a seasonal Scripture such as Luke 2:8-14 for Christmas, Matthew 28:1-7 for Easter, and Psalm 100 for Thanksgiving. Depending on the ages of the children, it took from two to six weeks to memorize such a section.

Our method was to read the Scripture through once every day. That's all. Each person (even the preschoolers who couldn't read) would have his own Bible open. Then we read the Scripture passage through slowly and carefully. I was amazed, as you will be, at how quickly they were able to memorize long portions of Scripture in this manner. If you begin using this method by the time your child is three and speaking fairly well, he will eventually be able to recite whole sections of Scripture.

An important note to remember: Put expression and excitement in your voice when you read the Word of God to your children. After all, it is an interesting, exciting, relevant story, so let it sound like one.

Sometimes I am asked, "When did you ever find time to have family devotions?" Well, until you have school-age children, you have the whole day to choose from. So I carefully selected the best time for us, set us a schedule, and stuck to it. Regularity is extremely important, because you are helping your preschool children establish habits. And when devotions are an integral part of every day at this age, your children will have very little difficulty in establishing their own daily devotions later in life.

SINGING

All children enjoy singing. And even before a child can sing himself, he enjoys being sung to. Music creates a mood. That is one reason why the songs for devotions should be carefully chosen. Notice the words of the songs. Many choruses convey an entirely different meaning to the children than that intended by the author.

I was made aware of this fact one Sunday morning on

our way to church. When we drove past the road that led to the city dump, one of our children spontaneously burst forth singing a Sunday school chorus: "Down in the dumps I'll never go." He had no idea that the chorus did not literally refer to the city dump. Remember, very young children do not understand metaphors, so it's important that they learn songs which are crystal clear and meaningful to them.

We started our song fest with action choruses. Each child would take turns choosing a favorite, then stand and lead the "others" (even if you are the only "other" person present) in singing, putting in all the necessary motions. Even the youngest can participate in devotions this way.

We also sang many Scripture verses set to music. I discovered that it helped our memorization as we remembered "what Christ taught and let his words enrich [our] lives and make [us] wise; teach[ing] them to each other and sing[ing] them out in psalms and hymns and spiritual songs, singing to the Lord with thankful hearts" (Col. 3:16, TLB).

Singing Scripture set to music helps to fill your child's mind with praises to God. (If your Christian bookstore does not stock a *Scripture Sings* songbook, one can be ordered along with singalong cassette tapes from New Life Publications, Inc., 143 Tuxedo Drive, Thomasville, GA 31792).

When you sing these Scriptures, choruses, and hymns daily, your efforts will be rewarded as you see your children grow in knowledge and understanding of the Word. You will rejoice as you watch their faces light up when "their" songs are sung in church or Sunday school.

STORYTIME

The preschool age is a wonderful time for introducing your child to Bible stories and Bible characters. If you can tell these stories in your own words, so much the better, because it's the easiest way to obtain and hold your child's attention. Have your Bible on your lap as you talk. (And, as mentioned in chapter one, don't forget to have a Bible map handy.)

Now you are ready to see and hear what God is saying: "For I will show you lessons from our history," he says in Psalm 78:2-4, "stories handed down to us from former generations. I will reveal these truths to you so that you can describe these glorious deeds of Jehovah to your children, and tell them about the mighty miracles he did" (TLB).

As you teach these truths to your children, God promises he will reveal himself to them.

If you are experiencing difficulty in telling these stories yourself, you may wish to read aloud from *The Bible in Pictures for Little Eyes* by Ken Taylor, which is excellent. (It is published by Moody Press, Chicago, Illinois.)

PRAYER

Your whole devotional period should lead up to this time of conversing with God. If you teach your child to pray conversationally, much as we talk to one another, prayer time will not be boring, but will be eagerly looked forward to. I usually begin our prayer time by thanking the Lord for something. Each child takes a turn speaking a few words of thanks; we go back and forth until each is finished. Someone may then pray for one of our friends, or for church people. Even pets and personal projects may be mentioned, each child taking "his turn."

Basically we move from subject to subject with each one praying at least one or two sentences on a particular subject or person. This method eliminates some of the impatience usually experienced by a child when he has to wait for others to finish long prayers before he can pray. Conversational prayer frees children to pray as soon as they think of something to say to the Lord.

Pray for specific things. How else will your child know if his prayer has been answered? In Matthew 21:22 (AB), Jesus told us to pray this way: "And whatever you ask for in prayer, having faith and [really] believing, you will receive." I sometimes wonder if the reason we do not teach our children to pray specifically is that we ourselves are not sure God will answer our own prayers, and we don't want our child's faith to waver.

But when Jesus speaks of faith, he means "acting on what you believe." If you believe what Jesus said about prayer, if you believe there is power in prayer, then your prayers will reflect that.

One day my daughter Trish taught me a valuable lesson about praying. It was fall, about time for school to begin, and I was concerned about her school clothes. At that particular time Trish had one Sunday dress and I had no money for school clothes.

One morning Trish asked, "Why don't we ask Jesus to send me some school dresses? There are five more days till school starts. I have one good dress. Let's ask for four more!" I'll have to admit, it was with great hesitation that I knelt beside her to pray. She prayed with confidence, believing the Lord would answer. And I began thinking of ways I could "help" the Lord answer my daughter's prayer!

Then Trish began talking about her "four new dresses." She said one would probably be pink, "because pink is my favorite color." The more she talked, the more nervous I became. The next afternoon when the children and I returned from town, Trish's answer was there. In our big red chair was a large pile of dresses. Nearby was a box with a winter coat and hat—and a pair of shoes just the right size. All of this was much more than I could ever have purchased. Trish's faith soared to immense heights. And as she picked out a pretty *pink* dress, she said, "Jesus did answer . . . now I want to thank him."

We hardly knew our benefactor, which didn't matter. What did matter was that God had put into that woman's heart the desire to bring those clothes to Trish. And she had responded. Trish had asked in faith. God said, "Faith is being . . . certain of what we do not see." Faith is acting like I have already received what God said he would give me, even before I see any material evidence of it.

Trish had done just that. And since she met the
condition of Matthew 6:33—Jesus fulfilled his promise
to her, as he said he would.

Times of stress or crisis are when your child's "Truth
and Consequences" book will be especially useful.
We found use for ours the night our neighbor's dog barked
continuously for more than an hour and kept us awake.
We thought of reporting the dog to the police. Then
someone turned to the promise: "He giveth his beloved
sleep" (Psa. 127:2).

We read the condition that must be met before that
promise could be fulfilled. It was: "You must live your
daily life according to God's Word, and must not be
living anxiously." We knew we were meeting the
condition, so we prayed, asking God to close the dog's
mouth and keep it quiet so we could sleep. Believe me,
it is much easier to pray for God to "feed the poor in
India" or "help the missionaries" than to close the mouth
of the neighbor's barking dog.

But we prayed expectantly. Moments later the barking
ceased. Our home was filled with excitement when we
once again experienced the power of God who is the same
now as when he created the earth.

Encourage your children to make their own "Answers
to Prayer" notebook. Of course, the family should have
one, but each child should keep his own record of
prayers prayed and prayers answered. It becomes very
easy to forget the ways God cares for us and answers our
petitions unless we keep such a record. Write down
the date, the request (or for a preschool child, draw a
picture of the need or request), then the date and
description of the answer. When discouraging days come,
lift your spirits by reviewing the record and recalling
the "great things God has done."

There is nothing that can change an ordinary, humdrum
life into one of joyful expectancy faster than seeing
your prayers answered. Answered prayer will bring
your child security and hope which nothing else can give.

I've discussed a few methods I've used to conduct
devotions in our home. Your ways will, of course, be
tailored to fit your needs. But however you go about your

worship, try to make each day's devotions a little different. Variety keeps the interest keen. You will soon discover that profitable family devotional time does not just happen. It takes special determination on the part of the mother to plan for it.

Some days your devotional periods will be spontaneous. But the most long-range benefit will be achieved only when these special times are well thought out and well planned. To achieve this goal requires much preparation, perseverance, determination, and prayer.

Another regular event that requires great determination in preparing for is the Lord's Day. I still remember that wintry Sunday morning when the Lord so vividly showed me the lack in our preparation. I snapped off the alarm and wearily pulled myself out of bed. Outside the wind was blowing fiercely. I shivered, dreading the prospect of getting everyone ready to go to church on such a day. "Why don't you just stay home?" a small voice whispered temptingly. I paused to listen.

"But today is God's Day," another voice said accusingly. "And you always get the children ready for school, regardless of the weather." I sighed and reluctantly moved toward the kitchen.

Upstairs I heard boys' voices raised in a heated argument, followed by loud wails from the baby's room. "Someone's awakened Alice," I grumbled. Everybody's tired, I thought, including myself. I should have put them to bed long before our company left last night.

"Where's my white shirt?" Terry shouted above the din.

"I didn't get it ironed. Wear one of Keith's."

Keith came into the kitchen. "I don't like Sunday mornings."

"Why not?"

" 'Cause, you're always grumpy, and besides we have to eat oatmeal."

"That's all I have time to fix. And I wouldn't be so grumpy if you children didn't fuss so." I turned my back and began scooping oatmeal into bowls as the family began straggling in one by one.

At last in church, I sighed in relief. It felt good to sit

back and relax. For a while my mind wandered, then
settled on deciding what I could fix for dinner in a hurry.
I believe we'll have hamburgers again, I decided.

"Prepare to meet thy God!"

The words jolted me back to the sermon. The pastor
continued, "We prepare our houses for company. We
prepare our meals to be eaten. We prepare our lessons for
school. We prepare our gardens to be planted. We prepare
for almost everything but the thing most needful—the
preparation for meeting God in his house. I wonder
how many of you came to church this morning prepared to
meet Almighty God."

He was right, I knew. But I resentfully thought of how
busy I'd been yesterday. We'd gone away in the
afternoon. Then guests had come and stayed late into the
evening. This morning my hands had been full, as I just
tried to get my family dressed and ready for church.

Right then I vowed that Saturdays would become our
day of preparation. And since that day—for the most
part—I've kept my promise.

Thereafter I saw to it that the children completed
their Sunday school lessons on Saturday. This was no
small chore, for it consisted of reading the lesson aloud
to each non-reading child, and listening to the older
ones read the lesson themselves. It meant teaching all of
them the pronunciation and meaning of difficult words
in the lesson, then having each child tell me—or the rest
of us—the Bible story. The storytelling part we saved
to tell and discuss during lunchtime, so each child could
become involved in the other children's lesson discussions.

After that I'd help each child with his written exercises.
I believe it's as important for them to complete their
Sunday school lesson accurately and well, as it is to
adequately prepare their schoolwork. Memory verses
were always reviewed until they could be recited
perfectly.

Sometime during the day each child who was old
enough was expected to polish his shoes and get his
church clothes ready. Saturday evening they received
their allowances and set aside their offering. On top of

that, I usually spent part of Saturday preparing meals for Sunday.

Early bedtime on Saturday nights was a must—I firmly believe that what children get out of their Sunday school lessons depends a great deal on how they feel.

I think we sometimes forget that it is not the Sunday school's job to train up our children. The school and teachers are there to reinforce the biblical principles we are already teaching them at home. And one of those principles (all too frequently left completely to the Sunday school) is that of creating and sustaining a missionary vision. This truth came forcibly to me once at a commissioning service when I heard a seminary president say, "Those of you who received the vision of missions as a child, please stand." Three-fourths of the group stood.

The man's piercing black eyes swept slowly across the comfortably seated audience until the silence could be felt. Then his powerful voice shattered our ease with these words, "Every home proclaims a vision! What vision is your home proclaiming?"

Mothers can create a missionary vision in several ways. One is the strategic use of maps. (We discussed map usage in chapter one.) A good way to amplify the map's effectiveness is to place a missionary's picture as close to his country or state as possible, attached to a ribbon pinpointing the exact location. Use pictures of only the missionaries your children know.

If they have never met a missionary, begin corresponding with one so that your child can develop a personal interest. By encouraging your child to become a pen-pal with an "MK" (missionary kid), you will enable him to discover new insights into missionary service. When your child becomes involved, he will begin to pray for missions realistically and meaningfully. His early, personal interest in a few missionaries will be of greater value than a general interest in many.

And to really help your children get acquainted with missionaries, there's no substitute for having them in your home: for fellowship, for meals, for overnight. I agree with J. R. Mott, when he said, "I know no university education that means more to a man than to sit at the feet of missionaries." So what if people have to sleep on the floor? Missionaries don't want to be continually treated as "company."

By opening your home and hearts to those who have been immersed in other cultures, you can acquaint your child with these great people, who will leave a lasting impact upon his life.

Missionary calendars hung beside maps became our prayer reminders. When we received communication from our missionaries, we noted comments and requests on our calendar and spent time in prayer for each request. When the answers to those prayers were manifested, we wrote the date in red beside the request. These calendars became extraordinary records of God's faithfulness as we noted and recorded the many ways God cares for his children.

Accepting the monthly support of a needy child through an agency like World Vision or Compassion can become another beautiful family experience of giving. I know of a family of five that supports a Colombian girl through individual faith pledges. Each child in the family, depending on age, pledges to give from twenty-five cents to $1.50 each month toward the total sum of $18.00. The children gather their "pledge money" from allowances and various jobs.

I was impressed by the active faith of twelve-year-old Lisa, who said, "Last week God did it again. My baby-sitting job was canceled and I didn't know where I would get my fifty cents for Maria. But while I was walking along, praying about it, right in front of me a lady's grocery sack broke. I helped her carry her groceries home—and guess what she gave me?"

I smiled. "Fifty cents?"

"Nope. Sixty-five cents. God said when I give to him, he is able to make it up to me and give me more than I need" (2 Cor. 9:8, TLB).

All of us are familiar with missionary boxes or barrels which are often nothing more than a collection of discards.

In Philippians 4:16-19, Paul thanks the Philippians
for their gifts to take care of his needs. He writes that
those gifts were a fragrant odor of a sacrifice offered
to God that he welcomes and delights in. And because the
Philippians gave to the missionaries, God promised
to supply all of their needs (another promise and
condition).

We must teach our children the benefits of that promise
by our example. Do our children see us giving to the
furtherance of Jesus' Good News—before we satisfy our
personal needs? Are the gifts we give the best we have—
or are they just the leftovers we don't want?

One fall I witnessed a scene in which this principle
was practiced. I was a house guest in a southern city
where I was speaking for a seminar. The lady of the house
had spent the afternoon with her son shopping for
school clothes. When they returned, Todd showed me all
of his purchases and then asked, "Which shirt do you
like best?"

I pointed to a uniquely stitched, soft blue knit.

"Me, too," he said, then in a matter-of-fact tone
added, "So that's for God. Mom, please send it to Randy."
And he picked up the rest of the clothes and left the
room.

I looked at Meg, "I don't understand."

Meg spoke hesitantly. "A few years ago, I visited
several foreign mission fields. One day while I was alone
in one of the missionary homes, I heard a knock at the
back door. A young African man, whom I had seen
working on the compound, stood there.

"He said, 'I am finished, but before I go, I want to ask
you if it is possible for you to give me one of your towels?'

"My immediate reaction was to look for something that
the missionary wouldn't want anyway. So I found a
well-worn, faded red towel which I gave to him, and
promptly forgot the incident.

"The following week as I was preparing to come back
to the States, the same young man knocked on the door.
He was on his way up the river to begin studying in the
seminary. As he left he said to my missionary friend,

'Thanks to you and God for the gracious gift of so nice a towel. While I was working I was talking with God about things I needed to take to school, and God told me to ask you for the towel. Your friend gave me the fine towel. I am praying that God will reward you both!"

Meg's eyes filled with tears. "I had given God only what wasn't wanted or needed. So I promised God I'd never again give him less than my best. Todd knows that Randy, who is in the mission school in Brazil, needs some shirts. Together we're learning the joy and satisfaction of giving the best we can give—our sweet-smelling sacrifice to our God."

Meg's story reinforced a truth I was coming to know: Each of my actions, words, and attitudes, my efforts or lack of them, are leaving a deep impression upon my child's character—as it is with you and your child. And the adults those children become will be a composite of all the impressions they have received . . . from us.

*I took a piece of plastic clay and idly fashioned
    it one day.*
*And as my fingers pressed it, still it moved and
    yielded to my will.*
*I came again when days were past, the bit of clay
    was hard at last.*
*The form I gave it still it bore, and I could fashion
    it no more!*
*I took a piece of living clay, and gently pressed
    it day by day,*
*And molded with my power and art, a young child's
    soft and yielding heart.*
*I came again when years had gone; it was a man I
    looked upon.*
*He still that early impression bore, and I could
    fashion him no more!*